P9-BYY-364

THE Rooftop Growing GUIDE

THE **Rooftop Growing** GUIDE

How to transform your roof into a vegetable garden or farm

ANNIE NOVAK

PHOTOGRAPHY BY
Naima Green and Jackie Snow

ILLUSTRATIONS BY
Annie Novak and Lauren Heanes

**Cuyahoga Falls
Library**
Cuyahoga Falls, Ohio

TEN SPEED PRESS
Berkeley

CONTENTS

With this book, as in a garden, many hands make light work. In the course of writing this guide, no matter the rooftop, I met passionate, hardworking, curiosity-driven, and compassionate people. This spirit of alliance and commiseration in our efforts is what makes this work so invigorating. I am grateful for the contributions of written words from Lisa Goode, Mark K. Morrison, Manuela Zamora, Stephen Orr, Arthur William "Bill" Shores, Orren Fox, and Ken Greene. For their professional opinions herein, my thanks to Amy Trachtman, Chris Goode, and Lisa Goode of Goode Green; and Joe Donnelly, Joe DiNorscia, and Peter Phillipi of Skyland USA. They were never sparing in giving a generous dose of advice. For additional expertise, thanks to Britta Riley of Windowfarms; Ashley King of New York Sun Works; Meghan Paska, author of *The Rooftop Beekeeper*; Michael Leung of Hong Kong Honey; and Mark Winterer and Brendan Shea of Recover Green Roofs. My passion for plants was born and

ACKNOWLEDGMENTS

raised at the New York Botanical Garden among colleagues I consider mentors and family, most of all the staff of the Edible Academy.

I visited, talked, and commiserated with a long list of generous green thumbs to compile the best (and worst!) of their experiences. Thank you to Eli Zabar of Eli's Vinegar Factory; Abbe Futterman of the Fifth Street Farm; Assistant Commissioner for Citywide Services Artie Rollins of the New York City Parks Department; Melissa Metrick of Roberta's; Erich McEnroe of McEnroe Organic Farm; Jack Algiere of the Stone Barns Center for Food and Agriculture; Helen Cameron and Jennifer Rosenthal of Uncommon Ground; Marjorie Hess of the Gary Comer Youth Center; Eric Dayton, Paul Berglund, and Aaron Manulikow of The Bachelor Farmer; Leather Storrs and Marc Boucher-Colbert of Noble Rot; Fritz Haeg; Lora Hall of Pizza Romana; Kristen McArdle of Quince Restaurant; Meghan Boledovich of Print Restaurant; Christine Aubry, Benoit Laborde, David Haddad, and Nicolas Bel of AgroParis Metro Tech; Courtney Hennessey and John Stoddard of Higher Ground Farm; Angela Mason, Stacey Kimmons, and Darius Jones of the Windy City Growers rooftop at McCormick Center Chicago; and Sam Mogannam, Patrick Mills, Calvin Tsay, and Liz Martinez of BiRite. For sharing their residential rooftop adventures, a heartfelt thank-you to Amy Lehman, Alison Lo, Lisa Ricotta, Rebekah Nagy, Agatha Kulaga, and Paula Crossfield. My thanks as well to Peter, Charlotte, Meredith, Hilary, Matthew, and Alex Rizzo, rooftop gardeners and family.

While I wrote this book, Shaun Dubriel, Dabney Gough, and Kirstin Sandblom all took a thoughtful and encouraging look at these pages. Emily Edmonds Langham and Michelle Warner were rhizobia for my roots, feeding me people to talk to. I am indebted to Fred Rich for sharing his rooftop garden, and generously giving advice as a writer, gardener, and expert in all things. He is a valued mentor for making a practice of cultivating the long view of green spaces far beyond the beautiful ones he expertly tends. My deepest gratitude to Jackie Snow, Naima Green, Lauren Heanes, and Lucas Foglia for their incredible eye for the beautiful. I feel fortunate to work with friends I have so much fun with and so admire. Happiest and humblest thanks are reserved for the sharp eyes, gentle encouragement, and gracious generosity of Kelly Snowden, Betsy Stromberg, and Lisa Regul of Ten Speed Press.

Each growing season, the Eagle Street Rooftop Farm welcomes student visitors, volunteers, part-time staff, and a dedicated team of apprentices. I am humbled to work alongside such generous spirits, energetic and enthusiastic about using rooftop farming as a tool to empower and improve our landscape.

The Eagle Street Rooftop Farm is a garden grown out of the astonishing generosity of Tony Argento and his sister Gina Argento, and the rich community that Broadway Stages nurtures in Greenpoint, Brooklyn. They have supported us every step of the way, and we—the farm, myself, and our community—would not be where we are today as rooftop farmers without them, quite literally. For this, they have our endless gratitude and profound respect.

My father, Brian A. Novak, would have gotten a big kick out of the fact that his oldest daughter moved to New York City only to raise chickens, bees, rabbits, and vegetables on a rooftop. Fortunately, he and my lovely mother, Rita, raised me and my two strong, intelligent sisters, Cat and Caroline, to believe that anything can be done and done well with the right balance of good sense and gumption. Thank you, dear family.

I'll be honest with you: when I was asked to cofound the first commercial green roof farm in the country, I thought the idea was completely nuts. For-profit vegetable farming is a challenge in its own right, let alone several stories up in the air. On my first visit to the future site of Eagle Street Rooftop Farm in Brooklyn, New York, I climbed the stairs with a strong sense of trepidation. On the empty, open roof, the wind seemed too windy. The sun beat down on the silver tar roof surface a full twenty degrees hotter than at street level. Standing on the empty rooftop, I didn't hear the buzz of a single bee, honey or bumble. I was familiar with green roofs, but primarily as passive spaces planted with drought-tolerant plants like sedum. I was worried that green roof growing medium—whatever that was—would be too nutrient poor and drain too quickly for growing healthy vegetables. Moreover, I love insects and microbes, and I imagined it would be challenging to grow plants in an isolated ecosystem several

INTRODUCTION

building stories up above ground-level worms and mycorrhizal fungi. Besides, there is plenty of soil on the ground, even in urban landscapes. Why would we put ourselves through the agony of dragging it up the stairs?

But looking around at the greater landscape of North Brooklyn gave me pause. I was surprised to see that our neighbor had a small but well-established container garden on his rooftop. Looking west toward the sweeping view of the Manhattan skyline, a twenty-plus-story apartment building had unmistakably flourishing trees on its upper terraces. I paced the empty rooftop with a growing sense of excitement. Behind me, the sun was climbing up over eastern Brooklyn and gently pushing away the morning chill. Below, a solid patchwork of flat and open warehouse roofs glittered in the sunshine, a carte blanche offering for our purpose. I felt my doubts fading, replaced by high-octane optimism.

It was going to be a challenge, but I was intrigued. I'm a die-hard "yes!" person, and this rooftop farming scheme combined everything I loved: food, plants, and people. There was a dash of politics and the opportunity to improve city policy thrown in for good measure. I started to read a book a day about urban gardening, gleaning what I could about rooftops by moving between historical accounts of urban gardening to new publications about the possibilities of vertical agriculture. New York City has a long-standing history of rooftop gardening, beginning at the turn of the twentieth century when rooftop outdoor theaters lavishly landscaped with flowers, vines, and trees provided cool green spaces as a respite to hot summer nights in the growing city. Rooftops weren't just for the rich, either: Jacob A. Riis, one of the more famous muckrakers of the twentieth century, described a fictional tenement whose residents establish a grape arbor atop their local gymnasium. (The fiction account is a well-polished version of a true rooftop trend. A photograph Riis took around the same time shows a rooftop playground near Coney Island crowded with residents happily enjoying the cool breezes off the Atlantic Ocean.) As the twentieth century marched on, residential buildings throughout Manhattan continued to install rooftop gardens. Architecture, horticulture, policy, and the technology behind rooftop gardening changed, but the desire for green spaces remained. From the vantage of my bicycle, I took note of the cheerful wave of healthy tree boughs planted high above Manhattan's streets.

In the fall of 2008, we met with Chris Goode, Lisa Goode, and Amy Trachtman of Goode Green, the design-build green roof company in charge of the project. Chris and Lisa Goode had already had success experimenting with rooftop vegetables. Their six-story building in Little Italy, New York City, featured a green roof and container garden that included a lawn, vegetables, espaliered fruit trees, and even chickens. My cofounder, Ben Flanner, was new to farming but had a clear vision for the venture supported by a business background. I grounded the project with an obsessive passion for plants as well as years of farming and farm market experience. Critically, we had the full support of a forward-thinking building owner, Broadway Stages, a television and movie production company based out of North Brooklyn. Brother and sister business partners, Tony and Gina Argento, had agreed to fully finance the installation of the green roof atop one of their soundstage complexes in the historic neighborhood of Greenpoint. It was the Argento's enthusiasm for the project and unbelievable generosity that gave the green roof traction, turning a pipe dream of a farm into a rooftop reality. The sound stage they proposed for the purpose was a historic warehouse building, built with the strength of solid craftsmanship in brick and steel, with flat, well-drained, structurally sound rooftops.

We were all excited to have the chance to grow hyperlocal fresh vegetables, with food miles measured in flights of stairs. Additionally, the rooftop farm, as a green roof, presented an opportunity to address some of New York City's principal environmental issues. The growing media could capture storm water, preventing overflow on our century old, overtaxed municipal sewage system. The media and plant material would mitigate heat island effect, when urban areas become warmer due to human activities. I was excited about growing people as well as plants. Volunteering and apprenticeships were a strong and valuable part of my farm training, and an important component of urban farming.

To the blackest cloud there is somewhere a silver lining, if you look long enough and hard enough for it, and ours has been that roof garden.

JACOB A. RIIS,
IN *NEIGHBORS: A LIFE
STORY OF THE OTHER HALF*
(MACMILLAN, 1914)

As public interest in local food rose, as a food purveyor and producer I'd started to feel the positive impact that educated consumers could have on shifting the food chain towards healthier food, better farming practices, fairer pricing, and enriching the local economy. A green roof landscape also created the opportunity to stitch together the archipelago of green spaces necessary for those less well known New Yorkers, our pollinators and migratory birds.

By April 2009—after a couple of intense, unusually hot early mornings hoisting the green roof materials up to the rooftop by crane and raking the growing medium into place—we had the country's first for-profit green roof–based rooftop row farm up and running. Eager to experiment, we grew over thirty varieties of crops to see which performed best in the shallow six-inch depth of the green roof growing medium. We meticulously tracked sales as we sold to chefs and at our own onsite market. I diligently recorded the weather, as in June and July a nearly sixty-day streak of uninterrupted rain sluiced down the drainpipes off the rooftops around us, compared to the moderate and slowly released flow percolating through the green roof system Goode Green had installed. We carried two apiaries for honeybees up the stairs and carried hundreds of pounds of produce down the stairs. Volunteers trooped up in increasing numbers, asking how. The media followed hot on their heels, asking why.

By the spring of 2010, our lives had changed as much as the roof. We branched out into other projects. Due to the international press attention the Eagle Street Rooftop Farm received, Goode Green was inundated with requests to design and install green roof gardens. Eager to focus on testing the profitability of green roof row farming, Ben Flanner went on to cofound the Brooklyn Grange Farm: over two acres' worth of rooftop split between two sites in Queens and Brooklyn. Furthering their commitment to modeling green business practices, Broadway Stages installed a breathtaking fifty-thousand-square-foot solar array on top of seven of their twenty-eight sound stages. For the Eagle Street Rooftop Farm, they ask no rent for the rooftop's use and generously finance the farm's limited but crucial seasonal irrigation. Thanks to these tremendous boons, the Eagle Street Rooftop Farm thrives as a community nexus, offering educational programming for local schools alongside the for-profit sales that fund the farm's operating costs.

At the time, I remember thinking the biggest shift in my life that year was simply that everything I felt passionate about—people, plants, food politics—was now growing strong three stories higher up than it had been the season before. With the benefit of hindsight and many more years of experience, I can say that the difference is richer than that. The ripple effect from our rooftop farm led to a national sea change that reimagined the possibilities of the urban landscape. Rooftop farming not only no longer seemed impossible; now it seemed inevitable. It is an incredible feeling to see what you love quicken in the hearts of others. I continue to try and share that sense of enthusiasm, empowerment, and possibility with everyone who visits the Eagle Street Rooftop Farm as well as the other green spaces I tend within New York City.

If you are reading this book, you have probably stood on your rooftop—or some rooftop—and heard the clarion call of that same elated omnipotence. There is something of the sailor's spirit in the view from a building's roof. The wind is in your hair, the eye-level tree canopy ripples like waves, and the blank slate of your newfound growing space is a freshly discovered island, full of thrilling possibilities.

It's good to have that kind of energy, because you have hard work ahead of you. You will find yourself climbing multiple flights of stairs, or riding up in an elevator in which you are the only person carrying a bag of potting mix, your flats of lettuce next to someone else's briefcase. There will be times when the sun dries out your crops or the wind topples your trellises, or you find that pigeons have picked away half your plantings. Sometimes the bureaucratic red tape around rooftops may seem worse than the stairs. But it's worth it. It is undeniably pleasurable, healthy, and (sunburn, sweat, and frustrations aside) rewarding to turn what was once *not* alive, thriving, and green into something that *is*.

HOW TO USE THIS BOOK

Throughout this book you will hear from professionals and green thumbs who generously offered their stories and tips for best practices in the growing field of edible rooftop gardening and the new frontier of rooftop farming. In your own moments of inquiry or frustration, exploring new techniques or facing sunburn and bee stings, I encourage you to research more about their sites or seek them out for guidance. I have done the same with my own mentors for the many years I've been growing plants and food crops.

This guide includes sections urging you to "Grow with the Pros." These explain technical elements of rooftop farming and gardening from the professional perspective, as well as important concepts and terms. In the "How To" sections are step-by-step guides for a rooftop grower. The "Up on the Roof" profiles highlight the work of growers across the country and internationally, with information about their irrigation, growing media, growing practices, and other replicable choices you can try at your own site.

In your rooftop garden efforts, you'll be standing on the shoulders of those who have worked for thousands of years in agriculture and for centuries in rooftop gardens. Your work will become part of the last several decades of evolving policy, practice, and professional growth in the green roof, rooftop garden, and rooftop greenhouse industry. This guide should serve as an introduction and springboard to an increasingly informative collection of books, websites, and organizations dedicated to the forward-thinking vision of our landscapes to include suitable rooftops as part of our green spaces, landscapes, and food system.

Finally, throughout this guide you'll be gently reminded to check your city's policy regarding aspects of installing, caring for, and using your rooftop site. Don't skimp. This advice exists for your safety and the safety of your rooftop. Because these rules vary between cities and are frequently in flux, the moments when you need to check your local regulations are mentioned throughout the text—and you should take it from there! For example, before you get growing, use a search engine and basic keywords to look up the requirements for parapet height, rooftop egress and accessibility, and compliance with fire code for legal use of the rooftop. You can determine if incentives exist for green infrastructure, including green roofs, white roofing, and solar panels. You can check the legality of rainwater collection, and if your municipality has hard or soft water. Before selling produce, you can determine the regulations around fresh food and packaged products or produce, and if this varies between private and publicly zoned land. You can check if it's legal to keep honeybees or raise chickens. To get you started, a full list of suggested questions can be found in the Appendix (page 238) as well as on the website www.RooftopGrowingGuide.com.

*I saw a man, an old Cilician,
who occupied an acre or
two of land that no one
wanted . . . he however, by
planting here and there
among the scrub cabbages
or white lilies and verbena
and flimsy poppies, fancied
himself a king in wealth.*

VIRGIL, FOURTH GEORGIC
(TRANSLATION BY
L. P. WILKINSON)

1

Why Rooftops?

In the spring of 2009, as we harvested the
first crops from the Eagle Street Rooftop Farm
with food mileage you could refer to in flights of stairs,
the United States was still in the throes of the
Great Recession. Many of our first staff members
and volunteers came to us after losing their jobs.
Rooftop farming was a fresh idea, and they
wanted in—and *up*.

They wanted to learn to grow their own food—knowledge that Americans, stubbornly, have spent the last century moving away from geographically and intellectually at the cost of our health and the health of our foodshed (the people, plants, and places that make up the ecosystem of growing our food). The questions they asked, and what we learned through trial and error on our rooftop and in conversation with rooftop gardens and farms across the country, shaped the content of this book. These are the brass tacks, the *how* of rooftop farming.

As for *why*, rooftop farms and gardens present a rich catalogue of benefits. They can be found on top of supermarkets and restaurants, supplying vegetables, fruit, herbs, and flowers to the customers and diners below. Rooftop gardens can grow above apartments and condominiums as private spaces and allotments, and atop senior housing, hospitals, and community centers as pollinator-friendly places and horticultural therapy gardens. Hotels use roof gardens as amenities for their guests. Universities can use rooftop gardens for research, and schools use open-air roof gardens and enclosed greenhouses as classrooms. These models are not limited to cities. Suburban and even rural buildings with structurally suitable rooftops can benefit from the additional green space. A rooftop garden or farm can make a view more beautiful, a meal tastier, and can provide income or pleasure.

Additionally, rooftop gardens have an ecologically imperative place in our landscape, the characteristics of which vary based on the system you use. Done well, a rooftop garden can serve to answer to aspects of the heavy environmental footprint of a building's construction. Green roofs, typically more so than container gardens and greenhouses, can capture stormwater in cities where soil is smothered by concrete. Green roofs address heat island effect, cooling down cities where the dark surfaces of pavement and roofing absorb, instead of reflect, heat. Open-air rooftop gardens of all kinds—green roof, containers, and vertical walls—can provide food and habitat for insects and birds, and green space for urbanites looking for an oasis. On the other hand, rooftop greenhouses are valuable in a four-season climate where the enclosed space can provide a source of fresh, local produce in the winter season when an open-air rooftop garden would lie fallow under the snow. Rooftop hydroponics improve our use of water in agriculture by growing a high volume of produce with a fraction of the irrigation usually required. The value of each system and examples of rooftops accomplishing these goals are presented throughout this guide.

Ultimately, not all rooftops are suitable for green roofs and gardens. But the shocking fact is how many are and yet lie fallow. For example, in New York City, where I live and farm, a study conducted by the Urban Design Lab in 2011 sought to identify all rooftops within the five boroughs of the city suitable for commercial rooftop farming. The buildings were identified with potential for greenhouse, container, and green roof growing by their height (ten stories or fewer), their ability to withstand up to fifty pounds per square foot of live load, having a rooftop footprint of 10,000 square feet or greater, and by being a building that was not in use for "heavy industry or noxious purposes." Even with the rigorous criteria imposed, the study cited 3,000 acres of rooftops that fit the bill! And that's just for *commercial* purpose, where the larger size of the rooftop matters. No green thumb can see a statistic like that and not feel the itch to roll up their sleeves and get growing.

If you're going to climb up to your rooftop to start your own garden or farm, get ready: creating a rooftop garden requires permission, practicality, and patience with both your plants and local policy. Your vision and determination is part of what will change an empty rooftop into a landscape. It's worth it. From the vantage of a rooftop, it's easy to see the future.

An Abridged History of Rooftop Gardens

As an agriculturalist, I find great comfort in the long lineage of best practices that precede my own work in the field—it saves time to improve upon, not reinvent, the wheel! The history of rooftop gardening, green roofs, and greenhouses is an especially innovative and rich narrative. Many incredible projects lead up to the 2009 installation of the Eagle Street Rooftop Farm, the first roof garden to take a crack at for-profit farming on a green roof. If history piques your interest, refer to Resources (page 239). To skim through five thousand years of rooftop gardening history, turn the page.

3180 BCE
Evidence of early green roofs

4000-600 BCE
Mesopotamian rooftop gardens

1384
Subirrigated rooftop garden, Italy

1450s
Green roof on slope, Italy

1519
Rooftop gardening observed in Mexico

1680s
Massive rooftop gardens, Russia

3180 BCE
Skara Brae, a settlement of sod roof and stone-walled earth houses, thrives in what is now Scotland.

4000 – 600 BCE
Mesopotamian ziggurats features gardens of palms, shrubs, and trees on their rooftops and stepped terraces. The highest of these temples (at 300 feet!) is believed to be the inspiration for the Tower of Babel.

490 BCE, approximately
Listed as one of the Seven Wonders of the World, the Hanging Gardens of Babylon are constructed for the pleasure of a homesick queen. A summary from 1 AD lists the construction materials as stone beams, dried reeds set in tar, baked clay bonded with cement, and a final layer of lead used to support the topsoil, trees, and people. Features a hidden irrigation system.

1384
The Guinigi family of Lucca, Italy, installs rooftop oak trees one hundred and twenty feet up in raised brick beds two feet high, watered by a subirrigation system. The garden is still growing, albeit with new trees.

1450s
Palazzo Piccolomini in Pienza, Italy, is designed with a rooftop garden above four storage spaces cleverly built into the slope of the hillside (still open today).

1519
Before razing the magnificent Aztec city Tenochtitlán in 1521, Hernán Cortés writes to King Charles I of Spain of the azoteas—flat rooftops—lushly landscaped with flower gardens and trees.

1681
The Kremlin in Moscow, Russian, installs a six-acre rooftop garden adjacent to a ten-acre garden of fruit trees, shrubs, and vines. Young Peter the Great launches toy ships in its thousand square foot, lead-lined pond. The gardens are demolished in 1773.

1764
Empress Catherine II of Russia commissions a roof garden above the Winter Palace. A formal parterre with flower beds, fountains, classical sculpture, and an allée of lilacs, the garden is still open above one of the finest art collections in the world.

1867
The Paris World Exhibition features a scale model of the Rabbitz Roof Garden, a breakthrough in roof gardening for its use of vulcanized cement as waterproofing.

1883–1905
New York City's first rooftop gardening explosion. The Gilded Age saw the opening of the Casino Theater at 39th and Broadway (1883), the original Madison Square Garden (1892), and the Olympia Theater in Times Square (1896), complete with a grotto, forty-foot long lake, and greenhouse roof. The adjacent rooftop, Paradise Roof Garden (1901), hosted farm animals—including two cows—in an effort echoed by the Astonia Hotel at 73rd and Broadway in 1904. Before the project was shut down by the health department, the Astonia kept enough chickens to keep its guests in fresh eggs each morning. The Waldorf and Astoria Hotels (1890s, on 34th Street) and Hotel Astor (1905) rooftops surrounded guests with food, iced drinks, and planters full of flowers.

1904–1922
Frank Lloyd Wright designs and opens the Midway Gardens in Chicago (1914 – 1923), the Larkin Building in Buffalo, New York (1904 – 1950); and the Imperial Hotel in Tokyo (1922-1967), all of which feature roof terraces as garden areas.

1867
World's Fair features rooftop garden

1883–1940s
Golden age of roof gardens

1970s
Earth Day, EPA, and FLL established

1996–Present
Cities legislate for green roofs

2000
First municipal green roof

2008–Present
Commercial rooftop gardening grows

1914

In Zurich, Switzerland, the Wollishofen region water filtration treatment plant is outfitted with an early green roof design. Above a concrete and asphalt roof, with sand and gravel as a drainage layer, a foot of topsoil from area farmland grows numerous native plants, including endemic orchids otherwise threatened with extinction.

1926

Le Corbusier publishes *Les 5 Points d'une Architecture Nouvelle*. He sees the roof garden as the fifth component of a properly executed living space, restoring the footprint of green space lost in the construction process.

1931

Raymond Hood, designer of the Rockefeller Center rooftop garden, publishes "Hanging Gardens of New York" in the *New York Times*. Today, four acres of green are still growing atop the Rock.

1938

In London, the 1.5-acre Derry & Toms department store rooftop garden opens to the public. For many years it is the largest rooftop garden in Europe (and is now owned by Richard Branson under the name The Roof Gardens).

1942

Union Square, in San Francisco, opens as the world's first roof garden atop a parking garage.

1971

Roof Areas Inhabited, Viable, and Covered with Vegetation is published in Germany. Germany pioneers the use of lightweight, vegetated rooftops using a gravel layer, a thin layer of growing medium, and minimal plantings.

1970s

Both Earth Day and the Environmental Protection Agency (EPA) are created.

1975

The Research Society for Landscape Development and Landscape Design (Forschungsgesellschaft Landschaftsentwicklung Landschaftbau or FLL) is founded. The FLL Guidelines continue to define terms, testing, and standards for green roofs today.

1996

Munich is the first city in Germany to require a green roof on any newly constructed flat or slightly sloped rooftop over 1,086 square feet. To date, one in ten rooftops in Germany are green roofs.

2000

Under mayor Richard M. Daley, Chicago City Hall is retrofitted with a twenty-thousand-square-foot semi-intensive green roof. To date, Chicago boasts seven million square feet of green roofs.

2008

Portland, Oregon, launches the Grey to Green Initiative, a series of incentives for building owners to install "ecoroofs." By 2013, Portland has 300 ecoroofs and 130 roof gardens.

2008

Uncommon Ground in Chicago, Illinois, becomes the first Certified Organic rooftop farm in the country.

2008

Gotham Greens, a large-scale commercial rooftop hydroponic greenhouse food growing operation, is founded in Brooklyn, New York. The following year, Lufa Farms opens in Canada.

2009

The Eagle Street Rooftop Farm is founded, becoming the first commercial row farm green roof in the country. In 2010, the Brooklyn Grange opens its first location, becoming the largest commercial row farm green roof in the country.

*Always try
to keep a patch
of sky above
your life.*
MARCEL PROUST

Assessing Your Rooftop

Transforming a rooftop into a garden or farm starts
by balancing what you want to grow with how your
rooftop is influenced by your region's climate and
your rooftop's microclimate. Additionally, you'll
need to assess what your rooftop can structurally and
legally support, as well as parameters imposed by your
budget. In this chapter, we'll look at what you can
do to assess your rooftop site, and we'll introduce the
professionals who can make your ideas a reality.

Assessing Your Goals

Being an ambitious dreamer is likely what got you up on a rooftop in the first place, and I will always be the last person to discourage that attitude. But start with clear goals. Goals are a framework of measurable objectives, setting finish lines for you to cross. Be self-aware and start where you are. Goals can always be reset.

Your schedule will also influence your landscape. A garden takes regular commitment throughout the growing season, with the occasional peaks based on the plant palette and crop choices, the weather, and the time of year. No garden—even the most self-sufficient perennial herb or sedum landscape— thrives without regular maintenance. In many landscapes, the dieback of plant material is a natural way to cycle nutrients, a healthy way to create habitat, and often aesthetically pleasing. On a rooftop, decay can trend toward being unsafe!

Assessing Your Budget

Whether yours is a commercial or private venture, throughout the year you'll run into expenses from as small as buying extra seeds to as serious as repairing unforeseen roof damage. Set up a basic budget outlining your anticipated needs. A roof garden needs growing medium, amendments, irrigation, repairs, and maintenance—and all that before plants! If you don't know what price tag to assign to these, start by listing each item; pri- oritize these, and then start shopping around. Do you need to hire an engineer? Rent a truck to pick up potting soil? Buy trans- plants? Design bespoke containers? Fix your parapet? Run an irrigation pipe up to the rooftop? Knowing what you've got cov- ered and what still needs to be purchased, found, or borrowed will help you keep track of where your resources are going.

If your dreams are bigger than your budget, don't be discouraged. As a young farmer, I was told, "Your network is your nest egg." I've taken this adage very much to heart. Your rooftop garden or farm is buoyed up by advice drawn from

A rooftop landscaped with hearty perennial plants and self–seeding annuals might take a few seasons to take off, but it creates an oasis that is fairly self-sustaining and relatively inexpensive to maintain.

millions of years of plant evolution, thousands of years of agriculture, and an abundance of green thumbs, professionals, and institutions to call upon in times of crises, commiseration, and joy. Bring to your project every available resource. Many of my favorites are used as examples in this book, and the bulk of the others are listed in the resources.

Assessing Your Climate

In our daily lives we talk a lot about the *weather*—this refers to the short-term conditions of the atmosphere. For example, your roof might experience a hot summer or a rainy week. *Climate*

Rooftop-Relevant Climate Assessment

You can look up your area's climate data by county. NOAA.gov and USDA.gov are good places to start. In your assessment of your regional climate, you'll want to include:

GROWING ZONE	As defined by the United States Department of Agriculture, your growing zone is a kind of shorthand catchall label for the information included below. A map of United States growing zones can be found at www.planthardiness.ars.usda.gov.
TEMPERATURE	Typically given as the highest and lowest mean temperature, in degrees Fahrenheit. You can also look up the record high and low (and the year of each). Informs what plants will thrive in an area.
FROST AND FROST–FREE DATES (FREEZE DATES)	Given as an average month and day of the last day in spring where the air temperature drops below freezing and the first day of fall at which air temperature drops below freezing again. Growers use this as guide to plant out seeds and transplants in the spring, or count down the days until frost will damage crops in the fall.
LENGTH OF GROWING SEASON	The number of days between the frost–free and frost date. Some plants have longer growing seasons than others; this helps growers make viable choices.
MEAN PRECIPITATION	Given in inches monthly and as an annual figure; refers to both rain and snow. Growers use this average to guide crop and irrigation choices for their area.
EXTREME PRECIPITATION	Given in inches, with the month and year of the extreme rain/snow event. Extreme precipitation can cause above–normal snow load and saturated media weight.

refers to long-term conditions. In the United States, climate data is available for free through the United States Department of Agriculture (USDA). Among other climate metrics, the USDA measures the dates and duration of below-freezing temperatures, days of sunshine, and average annual precipitation.

Understanding your climate will help you determine if a particular rooftop growing system is right for you. For example, an outdoor hydroponics tower system in Austin, Texas, can grow year-round, but in New York City's winters it will sit empty five to six months of the year. Your climate will also influence the plants you choose to grow, as well as how and when to grow them. Before heading up to the rooftop, here's what you should know about the big picture for your region.

At Higher Ground Farm in Boston, Massachusetts, mobile containers allow the farmers to take advantage of areas of the roof determined by a structural engineer to have the highest weight–bearing capacity. After the frost date, the containers are reorganized to accommodate additional snow load where drifts build up, influenced by the icy winds off the Boston Harbor.

Growing zone and frost-free dates. The United States Department of Agriculture created the growing zone map by dividing the country latitudinally by coldest average annual temperature, each a ten-degree difference from its neighbor. Additionally, the USDA created a list of the frost and frost-free dates to indicate how many days each zone stays below freezing. The two together tell you how long a growing season you have by the number of days between the average first frost-free date and first frost date. When you're growing annual crops, you can check the "days to harvest" against your growing zone's window of frost-free days to determine whether there are enough to grow the plant to maturity. Starting a plant early in a greenhouse or using season extension techniques at the end of a season helps to widen that window.

You'll often see plants referred to by their "hardiness" listed with a number, such as "hardy to zone 7" or "hardy to zone 5b." This indicates their tolerance for below-freezing temperatures and for what duration. This is particularly useful information when selecting plants like shrubs, trees, and perennial herbs and flowers. If you're growing a perennial plant outside of its preferred growing zone, you may have to bring it indoors during the colder months of the year. Keep that in mind when you select the plant and its container, or before planting it in a green roof or rooftop garden bed!

Average day length. The farther north (or south) your rooftop is from the equator, the more dramatic your long and short days are in length and brevity of light exposure. Understanding how many hours of daylight your roof receives and how it changes throughout the year will help you maximize your planting plan and the best place on your rooftop to put your plants. For example, on our rooftop in New York City, when we get into the long daylight hours of the summer solstice our vegetables seem to grow an inch a day. After June 21, as the minutes of daylight are stolen away each day, they turn their resources toward fruiting, flowering, and setting seeds. We know this from looking up sunrise and sunset times on the USDA website, and we plan our planting accordingly.

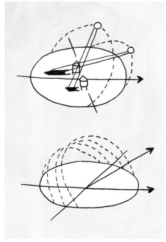

Throughout the year as the sun appears higher and lower in the sky, your rooftop's light exposure and shadows cast by rooftop hardscaping and nearby buildings change.

Additionally, the path of the sun across the sky shifts seasonally. If there are any large objects on or around your rooftop, such as air-conditioning units, water towers, or nearby buildings, the amount of light your garden will receive will vary throughout the year as the sun rises, crosses, and sets (in terms of your rooftop garden) lower or higher in the sky. Assess where nearby buildings, trees, and your rooftop's mechanicals will cast shadows and how long they'll linger at different points of the season. Since we can't change the course of the sun across the sky, aim instead to focus on controllable factors like plant choices. Note where shifting seasonal shadows fall across your rooftop, and select for plants that handle full and partial sun well or thrive in shady places.

Average annual precipitation. Climate data on average annual precipitation includes snow, rain, and humidity. The weight of your average annual snowfall (if any) will determine the limit of additional weight you can put on your rooftop. The inches of rain expected per year (and when) will guide both your plant palette and also your irrigation

An astrological phenomenon in New York City, during "Manhattanhendge," the setting sun aligns perfectly with Manhattan's street grid. For us, this signals the beginning of the end of our long days, and the time to begin preparing for the fall season.

system needs for keeping your crops properly watered. Keep in mind, too, that rooftop soils are generally designed to be lightweight and drain well. These types of growing media can suffer from nutrient loss in growing zones with higher average annual rainfall. Keep that data in mind when selecting your growing medium and outlining your fertilizing regime.

Assessing Your Microclimate

Now that you've looked at the big picture, it's time to scale this information down to the level of your site. The term "microclimate" refers to an area that has different levels of moisture, temperature, and wind than the wider climate area that surrounds it. The term has no implication of scale except as it is useful to you! For example, an urban area several degrees warmer than its surrounding geography can be considered a microclimate. A rooftop garden has its own microclimate distinct from the ground-level gardens below.

Common Rooftop Microclimates

SHADOW PROJECTIONS	Look for areas of the rooftop cast into shade by nearby buildings, trees, and hardscaping.
HOT SPOTS	Temperatures on a hot rooftop can rise, further influenced by reflective surfaces such as nearby building facades and heat-trapping surfaces such as brick walls or black tar-and-gravel or rubber roof membranes. On a larger scale, heat island effect can affect your roof. The large paved portions of cities; the heat generated by buildings, machinery, and cars; and heat-trapping air pollutants all contribute to heat island effect. (For example, in New York City, the temperature can rise 10°F higher than in its suburbs. Temperatures in central Mexico City can rise 18°F hotter than in outlying areas.)
DAMP ZONES	Even a "flat" roof has a slope. After a rain event, keep an eye on the rooftop for areas of poor drainage where ponding (water collection) occurs.
WIND ZONES	Wind has a major influence on the success and safety of a rooftop garden. The higher the rooftop, the harsher the wind. Assess your regular gusts for force and direction.

LEFT At this site thirty-four stories above Manhattan, the vegetable garden was located at the north end of the rooftop landscape to protect it from harsh winds moving south to north off New York City's Battery Park harbor—at the cost of being shaded out during the afternoon by the building's bulkhead to the west of the garden.

BOTTOM, LEFT At this rooftop in Brooklyn, the silver tar rooftop creates a hot, reflective surface that quickly dries up the garden's containers. During the hotter months of the year, plants show signs of stress, such as early flowering.

BOTTOM, RIGHT On this six-story rooftop in Bronxville, New York, a high parapet dramatically decreases the effect of wind. Parapets, screens, and rooftop trees can provide protection on the leeward side for a distance of five times the height of the screen, and a sheltering effect for up to ten times that height.

TOP At this green roof garden in Manhattan, an area of rooftop with a proclivity toward ponding was designed to the landscape's advantage and planted out with a thirsty lawn.

BOTTOM Microclimates can change seasonally, and circumstances can change, too. For example, at this rooftop site in Boston, if this neighbor's tree is felled, sun and wind exposure could increase dramatically.

Assessing Rooftop Sun Exposure

In addition to identifying microclimates on your rooftop, it's important to understand how much light your plants truly receive on your roof. A plant's growing preferences are often described as "shade-loving" or "partial sun" tolerant. Try not to misjudge the amount of light your plants will receive. Nearby buildings with reflective surfaces and the surface of the rooftop itself can cause a significant amount of glare. Even a low parapet wall can cast shade. Most gardeners are optimistically overgenerous in evaluating light exposure, assuming that a rooftop above it all inherently receives full sun. But you'd be surprised!

A basic assessment of your rooftop's sun exposure can be made by looking at the sharpness of your shadow on the roof. At different points in the day, stand where you'd like to grow your plants and take a look at your shadow.

- Crisp shadow = Full sun
- Diffuse shadow = Bright shade
- Hazy shadow = Medium shade
- No shadow = Deep shade

Landscape designers, horticulturalists, and nerds like me love to use even more accurate and technical ways to assess light. This is particularly useful when planting long-term perennials (before committing them to a microclimate with too much sun or shade), when designing a greenhouse structure, or when making a choice between plants that have distinct sun or shade preferences. For example, you can assess the amount and quality of light plants receive as measured by the intensity (or irradiance), the duration of the daily light period, and the spectrum, or wavelength composition, of the light source. The intensity of light on a given square foot is measured in foot-candles. Light on a full-sun rooftop has an intensity of 10,000 foot-candles. An overcast day has an intensity of 1,000 foot-candles. By comparison,

How to Measure the Light Your Plants Receive

If you don't own a light meter but you do own a digital camera with manual settings, there's a simple way to determine how many foot-candles of light your plants receive.

- Set the ASA at 200.
- Set the shutter speed at 1/125 of a second.
- Aim the camera at the light source (the sun or the plant lights).
- Dial the f-stop to the proper photo exposure.
- The f-stop can be translated to foot-candle values as follows:

F-STOP	FOOT-CANDLE
2.8	32
4	64
5.6	125
8	250
15	1,000
22	2,000

a plant growing on a windowsill indoors typically receives only 100–750 foot-candles (or in the best south-facing windows, up to 5,000). While most indoor houseplants can grow at 250–500 foot-candles, edible crops (particularly fruiting crops, such as tomatoes) need at least 1,000 foot-candles (and a longer period of exposure to light) to thrive.

Measuring Light Exposure

SUN EXPOSURE	DESCRIBED AS	FOOT–CANDLES VALUE
Full sun	6+ hours of direct light	10,000+ FC
Partial sun/partial shade	Multiple hours of both direct and indirect light	5,000+ FC
Dappled shade	Intermittent direct light, such as reflected and some filtered light	FC varies
Bright shade	Substantial reflected and/or filtered light	2,000 to 4,000 FC
Medium shade	Some reflected and/or filtered light	1,000 to 2,000 FC
Deep shade	Little reflected light, immediate dense cover	50 to 1,000 FC

Before you get growing, aim to answer the questions on the opposite page about your rooftop site. Keep reading, as in the rest of this chapter we'll dig deeper on what a professional assessment of your rooftop may involve.

ASSESSING YOUR ROOFTOP

Assess your climate

Growing zone: _____   Frost-free date: _____   Frost date: _____

Average annual precipitation (inches): _____   Days above 86°F: _____

Assess your rooftop

Describe your access/egress: _____

What is the parapet height (in inches): _____

What is the local legal requirement for parapet height (inches): _____

Describe the rooftop membrane/growing surface: _____

The weight-bearing capacity (if known) is: _____ per square foot

Assess your microclimate

Is your garden on a (circle one):   Rooftop terrace   Balcony   Other: _____

How many stories up? _____   Is there strong wind (from what direction)? _____

The site is (circle one): Full sun   Partial sun   Shade

Assess sun exposure

On a separate page, diagram your seasonal sun exposure (as illustrated on page 20). Below, note how many hours of the day your rooftop receives direct light, diffuse light (partial sun and shade), and shade in each season.

January–April	April–July	July–October	October–January
DIRECT:	DIRECT:	DIRECT:	DIRECT:
DIFFUSE:	DIFFUSE:	DIFFUSE:	DIFFUSE:
SHADE:	SHADE:	SHADE:	SHADE:

Assessing Your Rooftop

YOUR CHECKLIST

☐ What is the access point for you, materials and emergencies?

☐ Where and how good is the roof's drainage?

☐ What and how good is the roof's sun exposure?

☐ What is the condition of the roof membrane?

☐ Does the parapet meet the location's legal height for use and occupancy?

☐ Where is your water access?

A PROFESSIONAL'S CHECKLIST

☐ What is the building roof's weight–bearing load capacity?

☐ What access is there for construction and installation?

☐ What (if any) repairs are necessary to the roof membrane?

☐ What permitting, if any, is necessary to install or use any materials on the rooftop?

☐ If additional construction is planned—for example, compost bins or a storage space—what permits need to be requested, what weight load can be accommodated, and where on the rooftop surface can they best be placed?

A rooftop is designed, first and foremost, to protect the building below. As a green thumb, you've started your survey of the rooftop site thinking about how your climate and microclimate influences your plants and growing season. Now it's time to look at the condition of the rooftop and make sure the site is in good shape to take on the weight, water, and foot traffic a rooftop garden will add to the building's structure. To assess these elements, start with an understanding of your local building code and the legal requirements for the use of the roof. Next, take a look at the different components of a roof's anatomy and make sure they are in good condition. Finally, rooftop professionals can move forward on repairs, assessing weight-load capacity, and following up on the permits necessary for the installation of your rooftop garden or farm. Empowered with the right vocabulary, you can enter the conversation prepared to ask the best questions for the best use of their time. The following are some important items to keep in mind.

Parts of a roof. A roof is not a simple single component but a composite of materials designed to protect and insulate the building below it. You can, on a walk-through, do a visual assessment of the condition of the waterproofing membrane, flashing, and parapets. Having an understanding of a rooftop's anatomy will empower you to have a confident dialogue with a professional roofer or engineer about the state of your site.

The building's structural capacity. The weight a rooftop can support depends on components from its foundation up to the roof deck itself. The strength of the building's structure—its foundation, core structure, and the spacing and strength of its beams or columns—is not something you can judge just by looking at them or the blueprints. To determine how much weight a roof can support, you must consult a licensed structural engineer. The structural engineer will look at the most recent architectural drawings (sometimes

PARTS OF A ROOF

PARAPET. The extension of the wall at the edge of the rooftop, principally as a fire barrier.

FLASHING. Wherever the membrane meets an edge, drain, or vent, base flashing and counter flashing seals the edge so that no water gets underneath the membrane, potentially damaging the roof assembly. Alloy, lead-coated copper, stainless steel, and galvanized alloy are a few of many materials used.

WATERPROOFING. Prevents unwanted moisture (snow, rain, condensation) from damaging the structure below. Generally, there are three types of waterproofing: 1) Built-up membrane (assembled in place by layering materials), 2) Single-ply (one layer of membrane protects the roofing), and 3) Fluid-applied membranes (used most often for rounded structures and vertical structures).

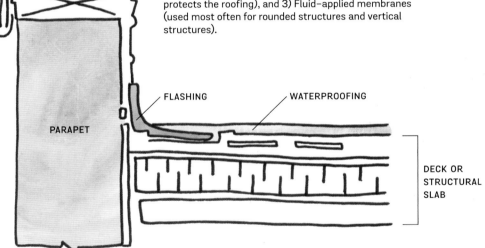

PARAPET

FLASHING

WATERPROOFING

DECK OR STRUCTURAL SLAB

THE DECK OR STRUCTURAL SLAB. The surface upon which the roof is constructed, spanning the joists or beams. Can be metal, concrete, or plywood sheeting.

ROOF SLOPE OR PITCH. Even flat roofs have slope (to prevent ponding and, where applicable, snow damage).

the building's blueprints vary slightly from the as-built updates) as well as conduct an onsite evaluation to determine its load capacity. This is done in part by examining the building's support structure and assessing what materials were used and their condition. From this, the structural engineer can provide the following:

THE DEAD LOAD CAPACITY	Dead load is the weight of all permanent features of the roof, including the saturated growing medium, containers, and so on.
THE LIVE LOAD CAPACITY	Live load is the weight of people and moveable objects. If a rooftop is accessed regularly, the Occupational Safety and Health Administration (OSHA) requires that the live load capacity of a rooftop withstand a minimum of 100 pounds per square foot.
THE SNOW LOAD CAPACITY	Snow load capacity is the weight of snow the roof must be able to support, as specified by local building code.
AREAS OF POINT LOAD AND LINE LOAD	Most rooftops have localized and linear locations where the weight load capacity is higher than weaker parts of the rooftop. Once identified by a structural engineer, they can serve as places for greater growing medium depth, or specific container design like longer raised beds (linear load) or larger single planters (point load).

The expertise of a structural engineer is necessary to calculate and verify the loads of a rooftop garden. However, you can get an idea of whether the limitations set by the structural engineer are being exceeded. To do so, examine your entire rooftop design. Determine where in your design the weight loads are potentially the heaviest and also the farthest from the columns and structural support beams. In that space, identify all the materials that will occupy a square foot.

Material by material, determine the weight per square foot. For products like growing media, containers, and green roof membranes, these weights are typically available from the product's manufacturer. To calculate an estimate of the weight per cubic square foot, multiply the per square foot weight by the volume of material used. The volume is calculated as the height by width by depth in feet. Do this for every material, then add them all up.

Again, this is an *estimate*. You can use this data to support a request for a practical load limit on the roof of a new construction, or to calculate whether your plan falls within the weight load determined by a structural engineer on an existing roof.

Identifying hardscaping and mechanicals. The preexisting hardscaping on your rooftop is important to protect. Hardscaping includes all permanent features on your rooftop. This could include staircase or elevator bulkheads, chimneys, water towers, and skylights, as well as mechanicals like air-conditioning units, fans, and vents.

TOP At this rooftop garden, all rooftop mechanicals are amply protected from growing media and encroaching plants by metal barriers and gravel fill.

BOTTOM Six stories above Manhattan, an oasis of self-seeding annual flowers and perennial berry bushes obscure without blocking access to the rooftop mechanicals.

Hardscaping influences the wind patterns, light exposure, hot spots of reflected or radiant heat, and frost patterns on your rooftop. Finding safe and creative ways to landscape around hardscaping can help extend your growing season, protect your plants from heat and wind, and beautify a rooftop.

Know Your Building Code

All rooftops are subject to building codes established to protect you, the building, and your neighbors. Here are a few common requirements to research for your local municipality.

Rooftop access. Rooftop access defines how you are allowed to enter and exit your roof and how many points of egress you must have. For example, many cities require that rooftop access be provided via a headhouse (a rooftop vestibule leading to a staircase) or a doorway from a building story at equal height to the rooftop. Sometimes the number of forms of egress can also determine how far the garden can extend from the headhouse or doorway.

Setback requirements. This is the specific no-build zone from the edge of the building. While this requirement is in part about aesthetics (preserving the street view of a historic facade, for example), it is also about safety. If the setback requirements of your site severely restrict your garden's footprint, you may be able to apply for a variance.

Parapets and railings. The height and design of the parapets (a perimeter knee wall) or railings used must meet code. Most building codes state that parapets must be forty-eight inches in height from the roof's walking surface for legal use of the rooftop. If you are installing decking or a green roof, both of which can raise the walking surface height of the roof, the parapet must maintain a height of forty-eight inches above the adjusted height. For example, a six-inch-deep green roof installation requires a minimum fifty-four-inch-high parapet.

TOP Many municipalities require that rooftop access be provided by a doorway from a building story at equal height to the rooftop. This is a headhouse.

MIDDLE Setback established by a fence installed by Recover Green Roofs, cleverly stabilized by weights rather than directly affixed to the roof membrane.

BOTTOM Railings installed at legal height on a superstructure at Uncommon Ground in Chicago.

For buildings without a preexisting parapet, or with a parapet height that does not meet code, railings are another option. Typically, railings must be installed with fencing to ensure that a child (or anyone else!) cannot climb them. Building code will dictate the specific amount of vertical force a railing must be able to withstand. To protect the rooftop, railings can be installed on a superstructure, such as a deck, rather than bolted onto the roof itself.

Know Your Zoning and Health Code

If you have any intention of doing rooftop farming, check your local zoning code before growing to sell! Agriculture is permitted only under certain land use conditions. Because of the rising interest in urban agriculture, many cities are updating their zoning code, but check what it says about rooftops and off-site sales. If you have your heart set on a site, often you can apply for a variance. Additionally, your local health code will dictate which animals are allowed (including chickens and bees).

If you live in a city where agriculture is not clarified in the zoning or is not permitted at all, contact your local councilmember. You can—and should—have a say in how rooftops are used, as well as local laws governing composting, beekeeping, green infrastructure tax credits and abatements, greenhouse use, and urban farming!

Assembling Your Rooftop Team

The installation of a rooftop landscape can include a big cast of characters. These professionals are grouped into what's called the "black arts" and "green arts"; the former are the professions that handle waterproofing, structural engineering, and project management; the latter are those who choose the growing medium and plants, and establish care and irrigation systems. As rooftop gardening and farming

becomes more popular, professionals of both skill sets are being asked for competence in both of the "arts." Many firms and companies will have in-house or commonly contracted partners they work with who cover all your needs. This is a great option if you like the company overall and they meet your goals and budget. It's a less appealing option if straddling skill sets makes for a superficial quality of work. Do your research and ask to see their portfolio. Seek out individuals and companies with a good reputation, positive reviews, and a solid track record.

For the safety and integrity of your rooftop, consider bringing the following professionals into the project:

Building owner. It is essential that you discuss the project with whoever would foot the bill for any damage. If the project involves significant construction, like a green roof or greenhouse, the building owner's signature will be necessary for permitting.

Structural engineer. For most rooftops, you also must consult a licensed structural engineer. It is their role to assess the amount of weight a roof can bear. Their assessment is often based on the building materials used; the condition of the foundation, beams, and columns; and the rooftop decking.

Roofing contractor. A roof mechanic installs, waterproofs, weatherproofs, and repairs roof materials. These range from the beams, rafters, and trusses that make up the skeleton of the roof to the tars, foams, metals, tiles, and shingles that cover the roof surface. Many companies aim to have professionals whose experience runs the breadth of these materials; others specialize. Many roofing manufacturers offer a NDL (no dollar limit) warranty on their roofing systems covering materials and installation for the duration of the warranty (typically fifteen to twenty years). A roofing contractor can be consulted to ensure that the rooftop garden does not void an existing warranty and that the entire team involved in the installation process follows the roofing manufacturer's specifications.

The Department of Buildings. Locally organized by municipality, the Department of Buildings (DOB) is the governing entity in the United States that reviews and enforces the safe and lawful use of buildings and properties following area building. This includes electrical and zoning codes, as well as local labor and housing laws. The DOB issues construction permits and handles property inspections.

Architect. The vocabulary of the architect allows them to translate building codes and local regulations and zoning and planning laws. Architects have access to building blueprints. An architect may also be most familiar with design prohibitions specified by historical preservation guidelines.

Landscape architect. As the name suggests, a landscape architect's task is to blend elements of the natural landscape into the overall design around manmade architecture. Professionals in this field have a wide range of aesthetics. Be clear in your expectations and what you value in your landscape. A landscape architect may work with (or you can alternatively consult with) a horticulturalist.

Expediter. An expediter or permit expediter secures permits for architectural firms and construction companies through a review process of blueprints and other construction documents, confirming their conformance with local zoning and building code compliance laws.

GROW WITH THE PROS

Mark K. Morrison

**PRINCIPAL,
MARK K. MORRISON
LANDSCAPE
ARCHITECTURE FIRM**

MarkKMorrison.com

Learn more about the professionals that turn a roof into a sky-high oasis on page 34. Here, the internationally experienced Mark K. Morrison offers "brass tacks" advice in an interview.

AN: What are the benefits of designing a garden on a rooftop space?

MKM: Rooftop landscapes are protected and safe and have great light exposure. When designed well, a rooftop landscape can have environmental benefits like stormwater retention.

AN: What does a would-be green thumb need to know to get started?

MKM: Every rooftop gardener should hire a structural engineer to do an analysis. A ballpark number for the weight-bearing capacity can sometimes be obtained by the age and type of building. Make sure the existing waterproof membrane is in good condition or will be replaced. Legal parapets must be maintained. It's always helpful when the same owner controls the space below the proposed green roof or terrace!

AN: What are some of the challenges in establishing a rooftop garden? Are there any particular to working in a city?

MKM: The approval process is always the most challenging. Availability of materials is essentially the same in or outside of a city, but it costs more money to work in the urban environment so budgets must be higher.

AN: Are green roofs suitable for every project?

MKM: Green roofs are more prevalent now than ever before. Research must be done to determine which is best suited for your project. I think the simpler the better.

AN: If instead of a green roof or in addition to a green roof system, someone wants to use containers, do you have tips on choosing what to go with?

MKM: The big decision in regard to specifying planters is between prefabricated or custom. Custom is usually more expensive but offers the greatest flexibility. You need to determine what you want to grow, which will determine the soil depth you need, which will determine the planter's weight. This will allow the load to be calculated, which then tells you if it will be acceptable or not, given the numbers shared in the structural analysis.

What a difference six years' of growth makes! Of the many stunning projects in the Mark K. Morrison Landscape Architecture Firm portfolio, the most beautiful and creative is the Battery Park Rooftop Garden atop the Platinum LEED certified Visionaire in the Wall Street neighborhood of New York City. Morrison and his team worked with the residence owner, Fred Rich, to scale up the preexisting green roof into a dynamic landscape. Rich was eager to demonstrate the variety and amount of food that can be grown in an urban rooftop setting. For example, Morrison took advantage of point loading above structural columns to plant a fruit orchard in open-bottom containers. These serve as a windbreak for vegetable beds in the garden's northernmost section, which the author tends. And what vegetables: as Rich writes on his blog (BatteryRooftopGarden.org), "The quality and variety of the food available for harvest (is) beyond every expectation I had when setting out on this experimental journey."

*A thing is right when
it tends to preserve the
integrity, stability, and
beauty of the biotic
community. It is wrong
when it tends otherwise.*

ALDO LEOPOLD

Containers, Greenhouses, Green Roofs, and Irrigation Methods

Rooftops can host container systems, greenhouses, and green roofs. Understanding the brass tacks about each will help match your goals to the possibilities available to you, as determined by weight load, local code, and budget. Developing a clear-eyed plan for the rooftop will allow you to stay on track with your objective, be it as a for-profit, educational, or private rooftop garden landscape.

Container Growing

Many rooftop gardeners start with container systems because they are readily available and can be easy to install, are temporary, and are affordable. Containers are available in a myriad of sizes, shapes, and materials. All containers should provide good drainage and good airflow, and a volume balanced between your plant's needs and what your roof can handle. Additional factors include cost and the aesthetics of the container's shape, color, and material—just to name a few variables! How each type of container functions on your rooftop also depends on your microclimate, the growing medium used to fill them, and your irrigation practices.

There are three golden rules to container gardening. First, the containers you select must provide good drainage and air-flow for your plants. Second, the containers must not damage the roof membrane. Finally, in consideration of the pedestrians below, be smart with your choices of container materials and placement. Keep in mind that if you live in a four-season climate, your winter rooftop will have drier soil and lighter containers for three to six months of the year. If a container is light enough for you to lift, the wind can lift it, too.

Repurposed beer kegs from the Six Point Brewery in Brooklyn, New York, are the perfect size for growing corn. Mulching with spent grain from the brewing process helps mitigate heat.

Container Materials

Container materials are varied. Cost, aesthetics, weight, and volume must be factored in when deciding which to use. I am always reluctant to weigh in on one container system over another, since ultimately I've found that any container of the right volume for the plant or plants it hosts with a good potting medium blend and irrigation practices will do just fine. The container system that proved this point best for me was in Ghana, West Africa. In 2003, I was working on my undergraduate thesis on chocolate agriculture at the University of Cape Coast. I walked to the university every day past a long fence hung with dozens of plastic bags filled with soil and vegetable seedlings. A woman came out every morning and slowly watered each bag using a two-liter plastic bottle. Despite her low-tech approach, her vertical garden had what it needed to

thrive: healthy soil and regular irrigation. By the end of my semester, the garden was so robust (and my enthusiasm so obvious!) I never walked by her garden without receiving a melon or tomato. Having seen such a simple system work, small wonder that today I raise a skeptic's eyebrow at the hefty price tag it takes just to pot up a plant!

When selecting containers, remember: potting soil dehydrates readily in small-volume containers. If your basil is baking in the four-inch-deep pot you purchased the transplant in, you might as well throw it on a pizza, stick it in the oven, and end its misery. Roots live inside that soil! Radiant and reflected heat from the roof surface and nearby buildings can affect a container's performance on a rooftop. A soil thermometer (similar to a meat thermometer, if that's all you have handy) will tell you how cooked your plant's roots are in the container you selected. Similar to ground-growing plants, soil temperature should stay between 68°F–80°F.

Finding the right size container is a balancing act between how well your growing medium retains water, how your irrigation system is set up, and how hot your microclimate gets. A good rule of thumb for most vegetable growers on a rooftop is to aim for five-gallon capacity containers and larger. If you are using a shallower container (perhaps

ABOVE, LEFT A mix of plastic, cloth, clay, and wood allows Agatha Kulaga in Brooklyn, New York, to experiment with aesthetic and horticultural variations.

ABOVE, RIGHT At Roberta's, a restaurant in Brooklyn, New York, recycled coffee cans with drainage holes drilled through the bottom are used to start plants. After a few weeks, they can be transplanted to larger containers.

Common Container Materials . . .

MATERIAL	BENEFITS AND DRAWBACKS
Metal	Used frequently for bespoke container design. Durable. Temperature of the container can be problematic; works best when mitigated by large soil volume.
Milk crates (durable plastic)	Portable, lightweight, easily acquired. Need to be lined.
Terra-cotta or pottery	A classic container material. Can be heavy and is sensitive to frost damage.
Plastic	Various plastics available. Look for those designed for outdoor use, resistant to sunlight and frost damage.
Wood (build beds, boxes, baskets)	Popular for bespoke use. Refer to page 45 "Using Wood for Edging, Raised Beds, and Small Structures" for tips.
Synthetic plastic, woven	Flexible in use, lightweight, easily acquired. Water-damage-resistant. Breaks down over time with sun exposure, and can have poor drainage.
Recycled materials (boots, shoes, small washtubs, retrofitted furniture, plastic bags, nylon stockings)	Results vary! Look for sun-damage- and frost-damage-resistant materials that drain well and are lightweight. Any materials being recycled need drainage holes.

. . . and Problems to Look Out For

POROUS, CAUSING FASTER WATER LOSS	HEAVY	BREAKS DOWN OVER TIME	FLUCTUATES IN TEMPERATURE
Unglazed terra-cotta	Terra-cotta	Terra-cotta	Terra-cotta
Peat pots	Metal	Peat pots	Metal
Wood	Stone or stoneware	Wood	Stone
	Wood	Recycled materials	

for quick-turnover crops like microgreens and radishes whose roots don't ever reach a container's full soil depth), aim for a larger diameter container. If depth is compromised, at least in a long, narrow container, the plant roots can take advantage of the lateral space. To find out what size container is best for your plants, experiment! Grow the same type of plant in several sizes of containers and keep track of how they perform. Before committing to a container style, do some research! Visit other rooftop sites and ground-level gardens. Read up on successful models in your area or a similar climate (paying attention to rainfall and temperature range).

As a general rule, I avoid using unnecessary amounts of plastic and plastic derivatives when choosing containers. Alternative materials (such as those listed in the tables opposite) have their Achilles' heel, but don't let that deter you.

Using Wood for Edging, Raised Beds, and Small Structures

Many rooftop gardens use wood as edging for raised beds and for structures such as cold frames, chicken coops, and decks. Check your local building code before using wood or actively constructing these features on your rooftop, as you need to apply for permits to do so.

When building containers for edible crops, avoid pressure-treated wood or plywood. There is absolutely no doubt that they do leach, and what they leach is not healthy for your growing medium, plants, or you. Pressure-treated wood can be identified by its greenish hue, or usually a piece of paper stapled to the board that reads "CCA oxides" or "CCA-C": copper chromium arsenate. A more expensive alternative is "alkaline copper quaternary ammonium compound" treated wood, which still leaches, but doesn't contain arsenic or chromium.

Untreated wood beds, containers, and rooftop furniture won't last forever, but there are smart choices you can make at the outset so they can resist decay. Look for reclaimed lumber, which has had time to age and won't be as prone to

At this rooftop garden installed by Recover Green Roofs just outside of Boston, untreated black locust wood is used as edging. At five years old, the wood shows no sign of wear. The mulch surrounding the framed garden is a recycled rubber material commonly used as groundcover in playgrounds.

UP ON THE ROOF

Edible Estates
ROME, ITALY

Founded in 2010

Third-story rooftop container garden

Total rooftop space: 3,575 square feet

Total planted space: 1,250 square feet

EdibleEstates.org

In the fall of 2010, artist and landscape architect Fritz Haeg was honored with the prestigious Rome Prize. As part of his year-long residency at the American Academy in Rome, Italy, Haeg designed and installed a rooftop garden on the Academy's third-floor rooftop terrace. The garden was planted exclusively in scavenged and found containers, such as wood produce crates lined with cardboard. An avid composter, Haeg started with soil harvested from existing garden beds in the Academy's back garden. Over time, Haeg amended the container soil with compost from a worm bin he built on the rooftop. Throughout the season, Haeg rearranged the containers to improve the various crops' light exposure, and the aesthetics of working with the growing plants' different heights and colors. Working with the Academy's chef, Haeg cultivated crops that suited the climate and honored traditional Italian ingredients: fava and borlotti beans, cucumbers, potatoes, strawberries, thyme, rosemary, nettles, leafy greens, and mint. In 2011, Haeg designed and installed a second rooftop garden in a greenhouse in Istanbul, Turkey, that continues to serve as an educational space, promoting the benefits of urban gardening.

rot. Use heartwood, the durable inner rings of the tree, instead of sapwood, the sugar-rich outer rings of the tree.

When you're shopping around for wood, the hardness, density, and weight of wood is described as its specific gravity. The higher the listed specific gravity, the tougher and stronger the wood. The percentage shrinkage indicates the wood's propensity to warp. The lower the ratio, the more stable the wood.

To make wood last, you can also be smart in your design. Sun, rain, and wind weather wood. For covered construction like cold frames and chicken coops, sloped surfaces will shed rain more readily. When fitting the pieces together, give the boards space to expand and contract. Use outdoor-friendly ceramic-coated decking screws, stainless steel or brass. Or use time-tested joinery like brindle joints and lap joints, or mortise-and-tenon joints. Leave the end grain exposed whenever design allows, as this lets the wood dry out after being exposed to rain, snow, or irrigation.

White oak, black locust, eastern red cedar, northern white cedar, and bald cypress are good domestic alternatives to treated wood available in most of the United States. If your lumberyard doesn't have these particular woods, ask what locally sourced alternative they would suggest.

At Uncommon Ground in Chicago, custom metal framing is used to reinforce wood–framed raised beds.

Vertical Gardening in Containers

To grow more crops per square foot, you can train them to grow up (or down, from elevated containers). Supported by a wall or fence around your rooftop, container systems are available as hanging "pockets" made of plastic, synthetic fiber, or recycled wool. Regardless of the system you use, these are still container systems, so you need to follow the same rules! Make sure the material drains well and the method you use to irrigate the hanging containers takes into account the difference in air and light exposure that a hanging versus roof surface system experiences.

Lightweight and easily installed, bamboo stakes and jute cord are great do-it–yourself trellising materials. A perfect teepee system, installed at the beginning of the season in less than ten minutes, later supports a bumper crop of lemon cucumbers.

For example, be conscious of the orientation of your vertical growing system. If the plants need full sun, position the growing facade toward the south. Check where and how the vertical growing system casts shade on the rest of your roof.

Where true vertical gardening (as described above) can be challenging, another form of vertical gardening works in the opposite, more traditional direction—from the rooftop up. Trellising systems, stakes, and cages can save space, increasing the number of plants per square foot that you can grow from the rooftop up. These systems increase light exposure, encourage good air circulation, and make working (pruning, harvesting) with your vine-type or climbing plants easier.

The shallow depth of rooftop growing medium can make trellising challenging. A teepee-style trellis of bamboo stakes, as shown on page 47, will hold better in shallow rooftop soil than a single stake. Squash, melons, and tomatoes grow well on A-frames. Pole beans, peas, and cucumbers grow well on teepees or vertical trellising against a wall. Using a sturdy bamboo and jute cord to test your first trellises is the most simple, lightweight, easy-to-store, and flexible design.

BELOW, LEFT A recycled plastic planting system of snap–on modules attached to a stainless steel hanging rail system. In addition to sedum, the gardeners have experimented with herbs such as geranium, verbena, and catmint.

BELOW, RIGHT The six– to eight–inch depth of the growing medium on the McCormick Center green roof prevented the farmers from traditional upright staking. Instead, a simple but effective frame–out is stabilized in supplementary poured concrete footers. Netting is raised as the tomatoes grow.

Vertical gardening, farming, and vertical walls have many iterations. Shown above are soil-based examples, as vertical hydroponic growing is discussed on pages 63–67. Here, fabric or plastic pockets create a "living wall," and bamboo or metal is used to trellis roof-level container and green roof crops. When designed well, vertical gardening helps good air flow (a good disease deterrent), and makes working with and harvesting crops easier. Pocket systems need special attention to drainage and irrigation flow (as this mossy pocket proves); staking and trellis systems should never damage the roof membrane. Metal tomato frames, for example, should rest on the surface of the soil on a solid hoop.

HOW TO BUILD A
SUBIRRIGATED CONTAINER

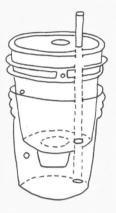

Many rooftop container gardeners have thrown up their hands about the ever-pressing need to water—and turned to subirrigated containers as a potential solution.

A typical container is watered from above and wicks up excess water as needed from a saucer placed below. Subirrigated containers are designed with an enclosed reservoir at the base of the container. Instead of watering the growing medium from above, you add water to the reservoir through a pipe installed at the side of the container through the growing medium. The growing medium then wicks up the water collected in the reservoir.

There are quite a few commercially available models of subirrigated containers. I recommend experimenting with them at first before procuring them en masse, as not everyone is happy with the results. They can become waterlogged, which both creates an anaerobic soil environment and adds weight load to your rooftop. To test if you like how subirrigated works on your roof, you can build your own first. You might want to consider making several at a time! This is a process that benefits from an assembly-line approach to make a few extra while you're at it.

Two 5-gallon buckets, plastic

1-inch-diameter copper or food-grade PVC pipe, 3 inches taller in length than the 5-gallon bucket

16- to 24-ounce funnel, colander, or cup of heavy-grade plastic or metal (The height of the funnel should not exceed the depth of the water reservoir minus one inch.)

Permanent marker

Drill with a ¼-inch drill bit

Jigsaw

Utility knife

Tin snips

Hole saw, if available

1. Drill a hole in one of the five-gallon buckets and place it inside the other five-gallon bucket. The ridges on the upper part of the bucket will keep the inner bucket raised above the bottom of the outer bucket. With the marker, draw a line or dot where the inner bucket's bottom rests above the outer bucket's bottom. (Putting a flashlight in the bucket helps, or holding them up to the sun so that light shines through.) Measure the depth of this gap: this is your water reservoir.

2. Measure the height and diameter of your cup, funnel, or colander. The height should not exceed the depth of the water reservoir minus one inch. For example, a four-inch-deep reservoir should have an internal funnel of three inches or less. (The drawing at left shows how the colander should not touch the bottom.) The diameter should be about a quarter of the diameter of the inner bucket, give or take an inch. For example, if the diameter of the inner bucket is twelve inches, the funnel diameter should be no more than four. Center the funnel, cup, or colander on the bottom of the inner bucket. Trace its circumference with the permanent marker. Using the jigsaw, cut this circle out of the inner bucket.

3. Measure the diameter of the watering tube. On the bottom of the inner bucket, about one inch away from the outside perimeter, use the permanent marker to draw its diameter plus one-eighth inch. Cut the hole using the hole saw (if you have one) or use the drill and the quarter-inch bit to puncture the circle, following with the utility knife or snips to clear it out.

4. With the drill and quarter-inch bit, perforate the rest of the bottom of the inner bucket, which now has one large and one small hole, with about two dozen more small drainage holes. (Pleasingly, it will now look like a map of the earth, moon, and stars.)

5. Using the utility knife or jigsaw, cut the bottom end of the watering tube at a 45-degree angle. This will prevent it from clogging as it rests on the bottom of the reservoir.

6. If using a cup or funnel (not a colander), use the utility knife to cut approximately a half-dozen quarter-inch to half-inch slits around its sides. This will allow the soil inside the inner five-gallon bucket and inside the cup or funnel to wick up water from the outer bucket's reservoir.

7. On the outer five-gallon bucket, use the drill to make two to four holes about one quarter inch below where the inner bucket rests. This will allow for airflow.

8. Finally, nest the buckets. Drop the water tube into place, angled end down. Pack your growing mix around it to hold it in place. Fill the cup, funnel, or colander with planting mix, then fill the rest of the inner bucket. Water the mix well to make sure it settles, then add more potting mix as needed.

9. The first time you water a subirrigated container, be sure to saturate the soil. Thereafter, you can add water through the watering tube, filling the reservoir instead. Wet soil wicks water well. If the reservoir and growing mix dry out, begin again by saturating the soil well, then returning to watering via the water tube.

UP ON THE ROOF

The Bachelor Farmer

MINNEAPOLIS, MINNESOTA

Founded in 2011

Second-story rooftop container garden

Total rooftop space: 3,800 square feet

Total planted space: 1,950 square feet

TheBachelorFarmer.com

Mixing container depths shapes your planting plan. At the Bachelor Farmer in Minneapolis, Minnesota, chefs Paul Berglund and Aaron Manulikow teamed up to care for a rooftop garden that supports their local food-forward menu. They use five-gallon buckets, kiddie pools, wooden raised beds, and plastic tubs, all drilled with drainage holes. Deeper containers like five-gallon buckets work best for long-term fruit crops such as tomatoes. Shallow but wide containers can be used for herbs and microgreens. Making lemonade from lemons, Manulikow and Berglund harvested their carrots as baby carrots when the taproot's size was compromised by the shallow depth of the kiddie pools.

Success when using shallow containers is due in part to using a rich potting soil mix. Manulikow combines peat moss with compost made from aged cow manure and adds perlite as a drainage aggregate and a small amount of gypsum to maintain the ideal pH for the vegetable crops. Over the course of the season, to keep the plants healthy and the potting mix lightweight instead of adding additional compost, the chefs use liquid fertilizers, such as kelp meal and fish emulsion. Featured on their menu are their top crops: cherry tomatoes, yellow wax beans, radishes, Hakurei turnips, chives, parsley, and borage flowers.

Greenhouse Growing

Rooftop greenhouses can serve many purposes, and their intended use affects their design. In a four-season climate, commercial rooftop farmers can use a greenhouse for year-round production, employing hydroponics or soil-grown systems to raise roof-fresh vegetables. For schools, the rooftop greenhouse can serve as a classroom, particularly valuable in the winter months.

These large-scale greenhouse constructions must balance at least three significant challenges unique to a rooftop site. One is the difficulty of access to the rooftop during the construction phase. Greenhouses have many moving parts, which must be craned to the rooftop or require extensive use of a freight elevator. Second, the rooftop microclimate is significantly windier than most ground-level sites. The greenhouse must be designed with structural accommodations for the vibration and uplift generated by a strong, steady rooftop wind. Finally, understanding the load-bearing capacity of different locations on the rooftop will dictate the customization of the greenhouse design and placement.

On a much smaller scale are greenhouse structures used as propagation spaces or for season extension. This includes smaller freestanding greenhouses with access for only a couple

On Manhattan's Upper East Side, Eli Zabar's Vinegar Factory rooftop greenhouses were a forward-thinking precedent to the commercial rooftop endeavors that followed nearly two decades later.

of people, as well as even smaller structures such as cold frames, and techniques like cloches, hoop houses, or using row cover. These are explained further in the table below. For each of these models, it is vital to check city code first to clarify which of these structures are legal and how they need to be installed. Many municipalities have strict regulations about greenhouses regarding fire safety, setback (how far the structure must be from the edge of the roof), permitting, installation, and materials used. Additionally, the size of the greenhouse and how it is used is under scrutiny in many cities, since a larger greenhouse can count as additional floor area space.

Greenhouse Structures

SYSTEM	CHARACTERISTICS
Greenhouse, large scale	The cost and permitting required for a large-scale rooftop greenhouse make them most effective in climate zones where year-round production or another use of the space (as a classroom, for example) makes it worth the expense and effort of installation. Greenhouses require irrigation, and for year-round production, electricity for heat and lighting. Large-scale commercial rooftop greenhouses typically use hydroponic growing systems for reasons explored further on page 61.
Greenhouse, small scale	Small rooftop greenhouses may be used seasonally to start seedlings by a minimal number of people, or as a growing space to protect and grow shoulder-season crops as temperatures cool. Because they are used during the shoulder seasons to start crops and extend fall crop growth, not typically for four-season winter growing, they require less infrastructure, employing temporary heat and lighting, if any.
Cold frame	Designed at the low, small scale of a garden bed, cold frames are typically used to buffer spring seedlings between greenhouse growing and growing on the open roof. At the other end of the growing year, cold frames can be used for season extension. Cold frames are typically manually operated and do not receive supplementary lighting. They can be heated using horticultural heat mats or heating coils placed underneath the plants.
Plastic cover/hoop	Various plastics available. Look for those designed for outdoor use, resistant to sunlight and frost damage.
Temporary season extension	To protect preexisting rooftop planting, rooftop gardeners and farmers can use cloching techniques and synthetic fabric row covers. They are flexible to use and affordable.

UP ON THE ROOF

Frontera Grill Rooftop Garden

CHICAGO, ILLINOIS

Founded in 2007

Fourth-story rooftop container garden

Total rooftop space: 1,500 square feet

Total planted space: 750 square feet

RickBayless.com

At the Frontera Grill Rooftop Garden in Chicago, Illinois, Bill Shores employs a custom-adapted subirrigated container system to grow tomatoes and fresh herbs for chef and owner Rick Bayless from June through October. The plastic resin containers are a uniform twenty-two inches long by eleven inches wide by fourteen inches high. Dissatisfied with the results of following the Earthbox brand–recommended growing mix and fertilizing regimes, Shores decided to keep the containers, but switch to quarter-inch spaghetti tube drip irrigation and his own potting mix blend: five parts peat moss, three parts sifted compost, and two parts perlite.

For Chef Bayless, Shores grows approximately a dozen varieties of tomatoes each year, focusing on flavor and production of fruit per variety, as well as staggering the days to harvest to lengthen the duration of each tomato's yield. Searching for tomatoes that satisfy this trio of characteristics has led Shores to delicious hybrid varietals, but often with academic names. When asked by diners in Bayless's restaurant below to share the name of the delicious tomato they're eating, rather than reply with its given name—typically a code of numbers and letters, easy to use for seed breeders but dull to his customers—Shores improvises a more romantic nickname on the spot!

Efficient design means two days of care per week is sufficient to maintain this highly productive tomato and herbs rooftop garden. To see the garden from above, turn to page 197.

Greenhouse Components

Rooftop greenhouses all behave differently based on site layout, size, and the materials used. Operational choices like heat, lights, ventilation, and irrigation will determine the crops you can grow and the seasons you grow through. Greenhouse materials vary in cost, efficiency, and appearance. Whether purchasing a kit, building from scratch, or hiring a design and install team, it's helpful to understand your options in order to make the best choices from the wide range of products available to the greenhouse grower.

Framing. The design and shape of the greenhouse is structured by its framing. Make sure the framing you use is suitable for your climate. For example, the size of the channel in the extrusion determines the thickness of glazing you can use. Greenhouses installed in zones with below-freezing temperatures should have an extrusion that can fit double or triple pane glazing.

Glazing. Glazing is the "skin" of the greenhouse. The glazing used affects the temperature inside the greenhouse as well as the quality of light transmission, which determines how much sunlight plants receive. Unlike the greenhouse growers of a century ago, who were limited to glass-and-lead greenhouses, today's growers benefit from a wide range of available materials, including glass but also greenhouse plastics (a plastic film), acrylic, fiberglass, and polycarbonate.

Budget frequently leads the decision on which material ends up glazing a greenhouse. You should also consider your region's weather, the glazing material's required long-term maintenance, and safety. Glass, for example, will outlast most other materials but is costly to replace. Plastic glazing is affordable, procurable, and easier to install. But many plastics (such as fiberglass) are highly flammable. Plastics scratch easily. About twelve to twenty years after installation, most plastics will also begin yellowing, which degrades the quality of light reaching your plants. Less-popular materials include Tedlar, siliconized cloth, clear Mylar, and ethylene vinyl acetate (EVA). If you're using one of these lesser-known materials, try to seek out a grower who is using them successfully and ask for their advice and feedback.

Glazing materials also vary in their insulation value and light transmission. The insulation value is expressed as "R." The higher the R-value, the lower the heat loss in your greenhouse. Light transmission is expressed in percentages.

Greenhouse Glazing Materials

GLAZING MATERIAL	R (INSULATION VALUE)	PERCENT LIGHT TRANSMISSION	NOTES
Glass, single pane	2 to 6	90%–95%	Wide commercial availability, good light transmission. Use tempered glass to avoid shattering. The higher the R-value, the greater the heat retention inside the greenhouse.
Glass, multiple pane (double to triple)	4 to 8	80%–90%	Triple-paned glass significantly lowers light transmission. As one adjustment, use triple-paned glass on the north side of the greenhouse and single- or double-paned glass on the south side, which receives more winter sunlight.
6-millimeter polycarbonate	3 to 6	80%–85%	More lightweight than glass and less shatter-prone; however, less light transmission and more subject to expansion and contraction than glass. Polycarbonate layers can be used with a 1-inch layer between materials to further insulate the greenhouse.
10-millimeter twin-wall polycarbonate	3 to 5	70%–75%	
16-millimeter triple-wall polycarbonate	5 to 7	65%–70%	
Fiberglass (clear)	1 to 4	About 90%	Inexpensive, but sags and bends easily under snow load. Has poor longevity and yellows over time. Generally not recommended.

Ideally, the glazing material you use transmits at least (if not more than) 75 percent light. To demonstrate how varied these values can be between glazing materials, the table on the previous page highlights a few examples of common greenhouse materials and their R-value and percentage light transmission.

The amount of natural light inside a greenhouse will vary based on the time of year, glazing used, and any shadows cast by nearby mechanicals and buildings. Many greenhouse growers use lights to supplement the shorter daylight hours of the winter or shoulder season. Before buying lights, know that plants respond to different wavelengths of light by producing different growth. Plants are deeply affected by the amount, quality, and wavelengths (measured in nanometers, or nm) of the color spectrum of light they receive. Think about your crop list before installing plant lights.

Air circulation is crucial to greenhouse health. Temperatures inside a greenhouse can skyrocket past outside temperatures in a matter of hours, easily frying your plants. Good air circulation prevents stagnant or overly moist conditions that facilitate the spread of plant diseases. As an enclosed

Plant Growth and Plant Light Bulb Type

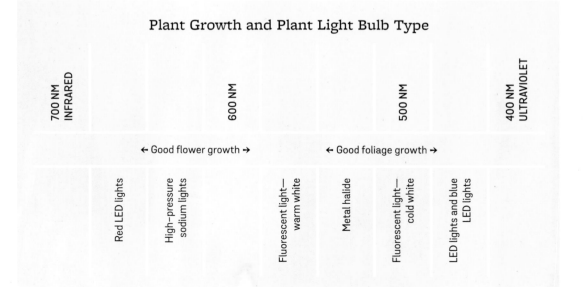

microclimate, greenhouses can quickly turn from an Eden to a nightmare of cycling pest and disease pressure. Both these problems are easily managed in a well-cared-for greenhouse, but quick to prey on plants in poor growing conditions. Both hydroponic and propagation greenhouses need a periodic deep cleaning. Toss or compost diseased plants. In propagation spaces and container-based systems, water wisely according to the plant's needs: cool, damp soil helps spread pathogens.

Greenhouses for Season Extension

Faced with the expense or permitting involved in installing a full-blown greenhouse, many rooftop growers turn instead to smaller, more practical starter options for extending their season. Before building any of these systems, confirm that your rooftop is a safe and suitable site for their use. Here are a few examples of greenhouse style structures used for season extension.

Cold frames are typically framed with an angled lid made of either a greenhouse-grade plastic or glass. The lower end of the frame should face south to receive maximum sun exposure. During periods of the year when the temperature fluctuates, the angled lid should be vented, or supported open throughout the day and lowered at night.

BELOW, LEFT One of Eli Zabar's Vinegar Factory rooftop greenhouses uses gothic frame double–layer six–mm plastic greenhouses to grow in–soil microgreens year round.

BELOW, RIGHT Cold frames can be used to harden off plants in the spring or to protect plants from cooler temperatures in the fall.

ABOVE, LEFT Built on top of shipping containers, the hoop houses at Roberta's are heated by the activity of the pizza oven and restaurant kitchen below. The greenhouse plastic is removed in the summer.

ABOVE, RIGHT Floating row cover must be securely pinned down. Here, bamboo stakes are used.

Hoop houses can be temporary or mobile structures. Few rooftops can employ a full-sized, walk-in hoop house. You can instead construct a modified, smaller, bed-size hoop house by affixing or bracketing the ridgepoles to the firm foundation of a raised bed or container.

The cloche, a word derived from the French word for "bell," is a micro-greenhouse. Traditionally made of glass, a cloche can be made out of any transparent or slightly opaque firm material, such as a plastic two-liter bottle. As with a cold frame, a cloche should be propped open or removed during the gradual warming of spring days. As with a hoop house, the increased wind of a rooftop can make cloching difficult. If using a plastic cloche, such as an upcycled milk jug or soda bottle, cut slits along the bottom of the bottle so it flares in a skirt, and use long landscaping pins to firmly pin down the flared strips. Any wind that can get underneath will quickly pick up and send the cloche flying, so use with caution.

A gauzy, semipermeable material with multiple uses on the rooftop (primarily as a physical barrier for pest management), floating row cover can be tented above crops to keep the frost away. For cold-weather protection, floating row cover is most effective when kept from actually touching the leaves of the plants below, as the moisture that collects on the cloth will freeze them as easily as if they were still exposed. On a roof, the wind will have at your floating row cover with gusto. Use landscaping pins (one gardener I know uses binder clips to secure the row cover to the wire they use as hoops!) to hold the material down.

Greenhouse Hydroponics

All hydroponics systems grow plant roots in water, not soil; use the water as a medium to supply the nutrients the plants need to grow and thrive, and circulate water to provide oxygen to the plant roots (often using a specialized pump called an air stone). To provide physical support for plant roots, some types of hydroponics systems use a medium like agricultural-grade perlite, expanded clay pellets, common pea gravel, or a fibrous material such as coconut coir. These open-air systems work best in a greenhouse environment, not an open rooftop.

As in any other plant ecosystem, the care and attention of the grower, available resources, and greenhouse or open-air rooftop microclimate will influence the health, quality, and yield of the crops grown. As with any other plant-growing practice, these systems can be done sustainably or wastefully, can produce delicious or tasteless cultivars, and can use organic or synthetic growing methods. Crop selection, nutrient sources, and energy source are up to you.

Many contemporary commercial rooftop farmers with large-scale greenhouses use hydroponics to grow their crops. The high yield of hydroponics satisfies the intense up-front costs of a rooftop greenhouse. In addition to the cost of the greenhouse installation, these operations tend to use heat and supplementary lighting systems to operate year-round in four-season climates, or cooling and venting systems to operate year-round in two- and three-season climates.

GROW WITH THE PROS

Jack Algiere

FIELD AND GREEN-HOUSE MANAGER, STONE BARNS CENTER FOR FOOD AND AGRICULTURE

StoneBarnsCenter.org

Jack Algiere runs a meticulously organized site. Highly conscious of the square-foot cost of growing in a greenhouse setting, his techniques focus on maximizing crop yield with the highest possible level of plant and soil health. To save time and streamline the planting process, Algiere employs simple systems throughout the greenhouse space and easily and clearly communicates them to his farm team. Although the Stone Barns Center greenhouse is on the ground, Algiere's methods work well on rooftops when applied to raised bed container gardens, green roof row farms, and raised bed–based greenhouses. To prepare the greenhouse beds for planting, Algiere uses a multi-step planting process.

First, the ground is lightly worked with a fine–tined bed preparation rake. This removes weeds and plant material.

Next, a broadfork aerates the soil to a greater depth while preserving soil structure and minimizing bringing weed seed to the surface of the bed. In the shallow media used on a rooftop, this step can be omitted or mimicked with a hand cultivator.

Next, a lightweight tilther powered by a hand drill aerates the top layer of soil at planting depth.

Finally, a seedbed roller smoothes the bed, presenting a firm surface ready for seeding.

At the Eagle Street Rooftop Farm (given our shallower growing media depth and the amount of gravel-like particulates in the growing media), we adapted these techniques by using a bow rake. Tines down, we loosen the growing media. Flipping the bow rake over, we use the smooth back of the rake to flatten the bed and prepare it for planting.

RIGHT Heat the soil, not the greenhouse. Hot water heated by a forced-air compost system adjacent to the greenhouse is channeled through coils on a table for planting flats. It is far less energy-intensive than heating the entire greenhouse space, and it promotes better germination rates.

BOTTOM, LEFT Floating row cover—often called by one of its product names, Reemay—is hung in easily undone braids. Floating row cover is used throughout the winter as a mini greenhouse hung just above the crops, and at key points in the summer to prevent pests.

BOTTOM, RIGHT To map his crop rotation planting plan, each bed is labeled and dated at the time of planting. This board is easily viewed and modified by the greenhouse team, serving as a central point of communication throughout the season.

On an island between the Bronx and Manhattan, the Five Borough Parks Department headquarters hosts rooftop hydroponics. Shown here is a five-foot-six-inch-tall system. When maximized at just over eight feet tall, forty-four plants can be grown per tower. With a two-and-a-half-square-foot footprint and proper spacing between the towers for air circulation, that's a quarter million plants per acre.

In addition to greenhouse-based hydroponics, open-air systems are popular on rooftops. These should be purchased or built as enclosed circulation systems to prevent rainwater from changing the pH or nutrient dilution in the water. One example of an enclosed circulation tower, the American Hydroponics 612HL system, can grow 288 plants at one time while occupying only seventy-two square feet of space. Keep the weight of these towers in mind: even a small four-foot-tall, two-and-a-half-foot-wide system can weigh 125 pounds even before adding the vegetables!

Each hydroponic system type is designed to grow specific types of plants. Although you can grow lettuce below tomatoes in a container garden, you would be hard-pressed to find that happening in a hydroponics system. The two crops require different structures, nutrient solution, supplementary lighting, and water pH to grow.

There are a handful of main hydroponic system categories, depending on your definitions: drip, flood and drain (or ebb and flow), nutrient film technique (NFT), deep water culture, wick, and aeroponics. These categories describe how the nutrient water is delivered to the plant roots. Within each category, there are various system types, and different companies offer slight variations of these.

Since the base of hydroponics is the water, regardless of what system you choose, test the water you plan on using to "fertigate" your crops (irrigate using a diluted liquid fertilizer). Hard water contains a good deal of dissolved mineral content, primarily calcium carbonate (sometimes you can see this on hot water pipes as a bit of crust). Soft water is very pure and low in dissolved solids. Distilled water is considered soft as well. Most hydroponic systems are designed for soft water. It is important to thoroughly clean all of a system's components every so often to remove any potential algae growth or contaminants.

Like soil-grown crops, hydroponically grown plants have pH and temperature preferences. In this case, instead of soil temperature, the *water* temperature (and temperature of the greenhouse structure, if used) is what matters. Additionally,

TYPES OF HYDROPONIC GROWING SYSTEMS

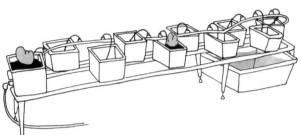

THE DUTCH BUCKET SYSTEM

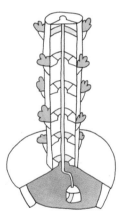

VERTICAL TOWERS

Hydroponic growing systems vary in cost, maintenance, ease of use, square footage needed, and the total weight of the system. You have to consider all this before selecting and growing your crops! Each has its pros and cons, as well as best plant (leafy greens, fruiting crops) for the system. Here are a few of the most common models. To learn more, read on—and turn to the Resources (page 239)!

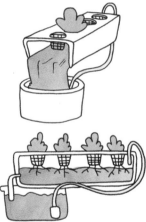

NUTRIENT FILM TECHNIQUE

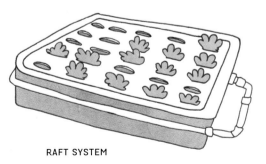

RAFT SYSTEM

the nutrient solution you use should be tailored to your crop choices. A good hydroponics guide will list the nutrient solution concentrations (PPM/TDS) best suited to your plants, which varies between leafy greens like basil and lettuces, or fruiting crops such as melons and tomatoes. In reviewing the list of crops below, you'll quickly realize why many hydroponic growers end up hosting multiple systems on one site, or putting together a single system that hosts plants with similar needs.

Hydroponics: Matching Your Plants Needs

CROP	GENERAL PREFERENCE, WATER TEMPERATURE	GENERAL PREFERENCE, WATER PH
Basil	Warm	6.0 to 7.0
Cucumbers	Hot	5.5 to 6.0
Lettuce	Cool	6.0 to 7.0
Mint	Warm	5.5 to 6.5
Parsley, thyme, oregano	Warm	6.0 to 7.0
Peppers (chiles)	Warm to hot	5.5 to 6.0
Spinach	Cool to warm	6.0 to 7.0
Strawberries	Warm	6.0
Tomatoes	Hot	5.5 to 6.5
Watermelon	Hot	5.8

UP ON THE ROOF

The Vinegar Factory

NEW YORK, NEW YORK

Founded in 1995

Third-story
greenhouse

Total rooftop space:
30,000 square feet

Total planted space:
24,000 square feet

EliZabar.com

A pioneer in New York City's greenhouse growing, the Vinegar Factory hosts greenhouses both atop its flagship store as well as across the narrow span of 91st Street (shown on page 53). Founder and owner Eli Zabar employs a variety of techniques to grow his crops, including the Dutch bucket system. The greenhouse's high ceiling allows for good air circulation while the material choice of UV-sensitive double-layer of six millimeter plastic helps keep the temperature even throughout New York City's true four-season year. Staggering the tomatoes on either side of the drip irrigation line allows for dense planting while maintaining good air circulation. Zabar's indeterminate tomatoes are supported by ceiling-mounted spools of blue trellising line. As tomato fruit are picked throughout the long greenhouse growing season, the old growth is lowered on the cable, moving the new growth—and tomato fruits—within arm's reach for harvest.

Spanning two rooftops, The Vinegar Factory's greenhouse provide tomatoes, basil, straw-berries, and microgreens to the popular landmark store below.

GROW WITH THE PROS

Manuela Zamora

EXECUTIVE DIRECTOR, NEW YORK SUN WORKS CENTER

NYSunWorks.com

A rooftop can serve as a growing space for both plants and students. Manuela Zamora shares the story of Sun Works Center's greenhouse installation.

The Sun Works Center is the first rooftop greenhouse built on a public school in New York City. It opened in October 2010 at P.S. 333 Manhattan School for Children, located on the Upper West Side. The process required dedicated parents, a team of architects, and structural and mechanical engineers to work together to convince their peers at the School Construction Authority (SCA) that this was a feasible plan. Since opening, the Sun Works Center at P.S. 333 has become an icon of innovation in science and sustainability education in NYC and beyond.

The greenhouse classroom uses hydroponic systems that are not only placed strategically for best light exposure and maximizing food production but also oriented to be easily accessed by the students. An aquaponics system or fish farm is at the center of the growing space, farming up to a hundred tilapia from fingerlings to adult fish. All the water used for food and fish production is rain-captured water. For crops, the students focus on lettuces and leafy green herbs that are ready to harvest in six to ten weeks. They are germinated in trays of rock wool, then transplanted into the aquaponics growing system. The students check the water quality in each system, monitoring pH and electric conductivity.

Every day, 150 students attend science instruction at the Sun Works Center. They have the opportunity to map major concepts that are critical to understanding climate change. The students learn first-hand how we can create a sustainable future.

The greenhouse classroom features a hydroponic raft system (left) as well as nutrient film technique (right).

TOP By employing a variety of hydroponic and aquaponic growing systems, students can grow different crops and compare results.

MIDDLE Students see their plants grow from seed to harvest, starting seedlings in rock wool to transplant into a nutrient film technique system.

BOTTOM The success of school gardens depends on strong buy-in from teachers, administration, parents, and students. The best school gardens make the direct connections between classroom curriculum and the rooftop garden space.

Green Roof Growing

Green roofs can host vegetable gardens, commercial row farms, native plants, flowers, drought-tolerant sedum, and trees. A well-designed green roof can mitigate heat island effect, help with stormwater management, and improve habitat for insects and animals. For the owner and tenants of the building, a well-installed green roof can increase the longevity of the roof membrane and lower energy costs. A green roof can increase the value of the building for the tenants as an amenity and for the owner as a marketing tool.

Green roof design varies; it is led by the need to strike a balance among the desired function and the structural capacity, roof slope, climate, and budget. In the design phase, a structural engineer will assess the structural requirements of the green roof and the structural capacity of the rooftop. As is true for all rooftop projects, this includes the dead load and live load. In this case, dead load includes the green roof assembly: the components of the green roof, the plant material, and the saturated weight of the growing medium. Live load also includes visitors to the rooftop, both for regular maintenance as well as expected capacity of a working space. In a four-season climate, snow load will also be calculated.

Both green roofs shown below (a classic sedum living roof, and an annual agricutural crop–planted rooftop) mitigate heat island effect, facilitate storm water capture, and insulate against extremes in a building's interior temperatures.

COMPONENTS OF A GREEN ROOF

GROWING MEDIA. Growing media, or green roof soil mixes, are available commercially. These vary in quality and composition. Each blending company has its own preferred recipe, drawing on resources available to them locally. Generally, growing media are made primarily of mineral aggregates such as expanded clay, shale, or slate, and secondarily of an organic material. Highly porous aggregates are lightweight, allow for good airflow and drainage, and add volume and depth to the soil without adding as much weight as other nonspecialized mix ingredients, such as sand. Organic matter holds water and nutrients.

FILTER FABRIC. Keeps the growing medium/ particulates from clogging the drainage system.

DRAINAGE CORE. Can vary in materials used, including egg crate–like mats, dimple mats, combination filter fabric/drain core/root barriers, and aggregate materials.

MOISTURE RETENTION/PROTECTION LAYER. Geotextile fabrics with capillary action properties are most often used. This layer also acts as protection for the root barrier and/or waterproofing membrane below.

ROOT BARRIER AND/OR WATERPROOFING MEMBRANE. There are several proprietary waterproofing membranes in the United States that have been successfully tested to be root resistant. If a waterproofing membrane is not inherently root resistant, a separate Root Barrier must be installed to protect the waterproofing membrane from root penetration.

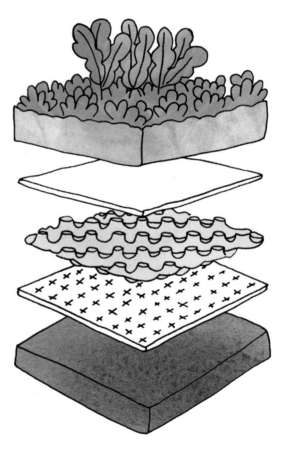

Modular, extensive, and a unique intensive system (with open-bottom containers atop a green roof system).

Green Roof Systems

SYSTEM	CHARACTERISTICS
Modular	Modular green roof systems employ shallow trays to hold the growing medium and plant material.
Extensive	Growing medium is less than 6 inches in depth. Can be installed on roofs with slopes up to 10 degrees and on steeper roofs with appropriate slope stabilization systems to hold plant material and medium in place. Saturated growing medium typically weighs 10 to 50 pounds per square foot. Irrigation is generally required during the establishment period of plants, then used only during drought periods. Generally, extensive green roofs are designed with nonedible perennial plants in mind. Often a limited-access space.
Semi-intensive	For rooftops with areas of higher load-bearing capacity, such as over internal support columns and along perimeter parapet walls, the growing medium is built up over 6 inches. For the remainder of the roof, medium depth is laid at 2½ inches to 6 inches in depth.
Intensive	More likely found on flat roofs with high structural load-bearing capacity, intensive green roofs have growing medium upward of 1 foot in depth. Saturated growing medium typically weighs 80 to 120 pounds per square foot and up. An intensive green roof usually employs an irrigation system to establish plantings as well as to maintain plant health throughout the year.

Green roof installations are described as modular, extensive, semi-intensive, or intensive systems. The current range of cost in North America to install an intensive green roof is $25 to $40 per square foot, membranes and growing medium included; an extensive green roof runs from $10 to $25 per square foot.

As the green roof industry grows, there are more companies available to work with. Keep in mind that equally as important as a low bid are the quality of their portfolio, good feedback about their work, and a design and timeline that meet your needs. As with any roof, the waterproofing membrane (or membranes) is typically the single most expensive item on the rooftop assembly. If the intention is to farm the roof, over time it's likely that one of the higher costs will be labor.

For much of their history, green roofs were designed as environmentally beneficial, aesthetically beautiful, but limited-access spaces. As green roofs evolve in design and use, the expectation of occupancy is becoming an increasing factor in the design process. If people are going to walk around on and actively garden the green roof more than a few visits for the installation of plant material, the design must provide up-to-code parapet height, access points, and pathways appropriate to fire code. Additionally, any rooftop mechanicals need to be protected. Heating, cooling, and air-conditioning (HVAC) equipment requires regular maintenance and should be accessible at all times.

Due to the low parapet height between these two rooftops, fall protection is required for anyone working near the parapet edge. A safety harness can be attached to the low cable running the length of the parapet.

GROW WITH THE PROS

Lisa Goode

FOUNDER,
GOODE GREEN

GoodeGreenNYC.com

Goode Green, a New York City–based green roof design and installation company, was founded in part as a response to environmental concerns presented by poor practices in urban storm water management. In 2009, Goode Green installed the Eagle Street Rooftop Farm in Brooklyn. Here, Lisa Goode explains her thoughtful and creative approach to reimagining the possibilities of a rooftop landscape.

For many years I've often heard the same comment from guests to my green roof: "I don't feel like I am on a rooftop!"

In the beginning, I took this as the compliment that it was intended to be. The roof was lush and varied and utilized materials that weren't commonplace among urban rooftop gardens (a lawn being one of them and a chicken coop being another!). However, in the twelve years since the designing, planning, and installing of the roof and the eventual creation of my green roof design and build company, Goode Green, I learned that this compliment was at the heart of what a green roof is capable of achieving.

Compared to rooftop container gardening or a greenhouse, a green roof can stretch the possibilities of what it means to "green" a roof-top. There can be a lawn surrounded by trees, because a green roof is a contiguous, built-up system that allows for soil almost everywhere. In creating this "blanket" over an entire surface, irrigation is used less and roots have a better distance to grow, ensuring plant success and maturity. A green roof is truly comprehensive in its use of every inch of square footage.

When the structure is strong enough, perhaps by adding support, this paves the way for an almost unending set of options for a green roof. I often try to convince people that the roof *can* be treated as if it were the ground. Options such as retaining walls, bricks set in sand, gravel paths, and lawns are all possibilities. Once an engineer can define the available loading, then I can determine the soil depths that in turn determine the types of plantings that can succeed. The success of plantings isn't always about the soil depth. A well-designed system in conjunction with suitable plantings can ensure a green roof that will mature for years to come.

RIGHT Underneath the gravel in the garden at top right, a continuous green roof system marries this landscape (a vegetable garden surrounded by berry bushes and fruit trees) with further sections of roof. Hens sheltered by a parapet wall are cared for by Goode's daughter, Charlotte. For more photos of the rooftop, turn to pages 17 and 24.

UP ON THE ROOF

NYC Parks Green Roof

**RANDALL'S ISLAND,
NEW YORK, NEW YORK**

Founded in 2007

Second-story green roof

Total rooftop space:
30,000 square feet

Total planted space:
30,000 square feet

nycgovparks.org/
greening/sustainable-
parks/green-roofs

Honeybees were relegalized in New York City in 2009, after an unnecessary ban on bees was overturned.

In 2007, the New York City Parks Department installed the first of many experimental green roof systems atop its five-borough building complex on Randall's Island. In the years since, the Parks Department has experimented with different growing media compositions and depth, membrane systems, plant material, and growing systems from green roofs to containers to living walls. These efforts, led by Assistant Commissioner of Citywide Services, Artie Rollins, provide a rich resource for students, professionals, and aspiring rooftop growers to seek out the systems that work best in New York City. (The entirety of their system is described on the website listed at left.)

To grow on the Parks rooftop, manufacturers and professionals petition for use of the space. If costs are covered and the project is deemed to be of interest to study, it is approved for installation. To date, the rooftop features thirty different models of rooftop gardening, from elevated planters to tray systems. Plant material ranges from sedum to New York City seed saved wildflowers to vegetables. The rooftop also hosts solar panels and honeybees and features an arbor with picnic benches where Parks employees can enjoy their lunch break. Surrounded by nodding flower heads and the sedum sections of the green roof, as prismatic as the sixteenth-century Ardabil carpet, the rooftop is an oasis between the crisscross of expressways connecting Manhattan and the Bronx.

RIGHT Native perennial wildflowers vary regionally. Shown here: liastris, coreopsis, and echinacea.

ABOVE Parks employees help care for (and harvest from!) the roof garden.

RIGHT A green roof tray system planted with sedum.

Designing Your Rooftop Space

To map out your rooftop, draw the site as seen from above. Generally, your design should include cardinal directions, drainage points, irrigation access points (or where it will be installed), access/egress points; the hardscaping, landscaping, and horticultural elements as determined permissible by local code and structure, shown in the table:

Design Elements to Consider

HARDSCAPING	LANDSCAPING	ADDITIONAL USE
• Permanent vertical growing structures such as trellises, living walls, or grow towers.	• Container or bed design, as applicable	If located on the rooftop:
	• For green roof design, raised areas of greater growing medium depth, framed or mounded	• Seedling propagation space(s)
• Furniture and structures (tables, benches, hammocks, raised decks)		• Cold frame(s)
		• Composting area
• For commercial use rooftop farms: Produce washing/packing area	• Permanent living elements, such as trees or perennials	• Material storage (for seeds, mulch, tools, etc.)
		If legally allowed:
	• The remaining plant material, including annual plants	• Rainwater catchment, greywater systems, water storage cistern
		• Animal housing or beehives

Rooftop Irrigation

Container, greenhouse, and green roof systems use water differently, but there are some common sense practices across the board. Responsible use of water is a must on a rooftop. Excessive irrigation isn't just environmentally irresponsible; it can lead to nutrient loss and anaerobic soil conditions. For this reason, many growers are strategic in employing conservative watering methods. Aim to water early in the day (not midday), low to the soil, and when the plants need it most throughout your day, week, and season—not as a regular habit, but as a practice based on observation and good timing.

Hand Watering

Despite the vital and necessary role water plays in the health of our edible plant palette, overwatering is just as much a cause of mortality as underwatering, if not more so. It's important to remember two very simple facts about your plants: plants should be watered only when they need it, and not all plants prefer the same amount of water.

On a hot, dry rooftop, plants can send confusing signals about needing water. While a flaccid stem and curled or wilting leaves may look like signs of a thirsty plant, those are also a normal symptom of midday heat or a myriad of plant diseases. To determine if it's an irrigation issue, check below the surface of the soil. The surface is likely to be dry, since on a sunny rooftop soil surface moisture evaporates easily. Stick your finger down past your second knuckle in the soil next to the plant roots. When you take your finger out, is it moist and lightly freckled with soil? Or does it feel chalky and dry all the way to your fingertip? If the soil feels truly dry, water well. Water until the soil is fully saturated, and then take a break on watering until it is just about to dry out again. This method of deep watering encourages deep and widespread ancillary roots. Plants are only as good at absorbing soil nutrients as enabled by their root surface area and supporting fungal networks. The growth of both of these systems depends on a good watering regime. For most vegetable crops, the ideal soil should feel similar to the delicious inside of a fresh-baked brownie: moist, but not wet, and springy in texture.

Hand-watering using a hose. This is a practical option for sites with a container or bed design too separated for a drip system. Watering by hand is useful when first establishing seeds or transplants, which may be growing too far from the drip line to get the water they need or may need a different amount of water from the plants around them. When intercropping, for example, while larger, established plants make

The soil surface may be dry, while the roots are wet. Go below the surface to check if your plants need water.

The vast majority of garden hoses are made of polyvinyl chloride (PVC), which leaches lead. Look for PVC–free hoses for edible crops.

Size matters for a watering can.

use of the drip irrigation, seeds sown between them may additionally need overhead watering to germinate.

Before purchasing a hose, measure the distance between your water source (spigot) and the farthest plant you'll be irrigating. Hoses come in standard lengths (such as twenty-five and fifty feet). Purchase the length appropriate for your site. A hose wheel will keep the hose coiled and kink-free. Hoses vary in material. Sun exposure and heat will quickly wear out a hose. If using a hose to irrigate food crops, look for ones free of lead and PVC. In addition to asking the garden supply company you're working with for a hose that meets these standards, you can seek out a hose specifically suitable for providing potable water. These are available through marine supply stores.

Hand-watering using a can. Watering cans come in different weights and sizes and with various roses—that's the part of the watering can that fits over the spout and breaks the stream of water into a finer sprinkle. The rose should distribute water at the rate and droplet size appropriate for the job: smaller "fine" perforations on a rose are gentle for watering seedlings you don't want to wash out, while larger "coarse" holes work better when fertilizing maturing plants with compost tea. Select a watering can that won't be too heavy to carry when it's full but large enough to make trips to the spigot worth the time. For some, it's easier to carry two one-gallon watering cans than one two-gallon can. The spout length and volume of water your watering can holds affects its balance and your ease of use. You'll feel it in your shoulders if you don't have right tool for the job! Although metal cans are slightly heavier and more prone to dents, I prefer them for their longevity. Haws, a British company that's been manufacturing watering cans since the 1880s, makes fine watering cans that last decades.

UP ON THE ROOF

The Noble Rot Rooftop Garden

PORTLAND, OREGON

Founded in 2006

Fourth-story green roof container garden

Total rooftop space: 2,100 square feet

Total planted space: 1,800 square feet

NobleRotPdx.com/web/garden

Urban-Ag-Solutions.com

Portland, Oregon is a long-standing domestic leader in green roofs—or bioroofs, as they are called in Stumptown. On the rooftop of acclaimed restaurant and wine bar Noble Rot, owner and chef Leather Storrs works with Marc Boucher-Colbert of Urban Ag Solutions to seek out unique crops to offer the diners below.

The rooftop is a mixture of green roof and container garden. Initially, Boucher-Colbert swapped out the green roof sedum to grow edible crops, but he found the growing medium too nutrient-poor for success with vegetables. After a few seasons of disappointing results, Boucher-Colbert decided that wherever the green roof could handle the weight he would amend the growing medium with aged manures, compost, greensand, and rock phosphate. Compiling a list of perennial plants that could grow well in these conditions, he planted Mediterranean herbs, rhubarb, and blueberries. The remaining central section of the garden is a combination of forty-two-inch-high raised beds (easy to work with at standing height), and raised beds built directly above a protective membrane on the rooftop (as shown in the photo, left).

One challenge Boucher-Colbert tackled when modifying the roof-top garden was deciding whether to switch from the originally installed drip irrigation system to hand watering the central section of the rooftop garden occupied by annual plants. Over the years of rotating a wide variety of crops in and out of the beds, Boucher-Colbert noted that drip irrigation systems make changing annual crops challenging. The spacing between different crops and their range of irrigation needs is better suited to hand watering with a hose. Hand watering also slows him down, allowing him to keep an eye out for the subtle (or not so subtle!) signs of plant stress, disease, and pest problems.

ABOVE Established row crops (particularly in large beds or green roof systems) are perfect candidates for drip line irrigation. Drip line is rolled up and stored away at below–freezing temperatures.

BELOW Based on weight, these rain barrels were installed at ground level underneath the staircase leading up to the rooftop garden.

Drip Irrigation

Many generalist gardening companies carry easily set up drip system kits. But as with everything, from seed sowing to greenhouses, there is an abundance of customizable options as well. If time allows, look into these rather than going with a seemingly simple choice. You can more easily tailor the system to your site, and likely save some money, too.

The photos and captions shown here illustrate some of the styles and systems available. Many of the green roof row farms and container row farms featured in this book use drip line irrigation, while the container gardens favored spaghetti emitters. Go "Up on the Roof" with Noble Rot (page 81) and the Gary Comer Youth Center (page 84) to learn more!

Rainwater Irrigation

Rainwater collection is a great idea, but there are a few things to keep in mind. First, check that rainwater collection is legal, and confirm that it can be used to irrigate the types of plants (edible, ornamental) that you're growing. Examine the surfaces from which the water runoff is gathered. Damaged roof membranes can leach, and are not an ideal surface for rainwater collection for edible crops. Next, you must determine that your placement of the rain barrel is a location that can handle the weight. Rainwater weighs about 8.33 pounds per gallon. Empty, a 55-gallon rain barrel weighs 20 pounds; when full, the same 55-gallon rain barrel weighs 450 pounds! If your site is suitable, look for an even, flat surface for the placement for the rain barrel and its stand. Use a level to triple-check this! Finally, if you live in a climate with temperatures that drop below freezing, you should also determine the empty rain barrel's winter placement to make sure it won't blow away or crack. Storing your hoses inside the rain barrel in the winter makes a good anchor, but rooftop winds are a fierce force. Additional weight or protection may be necessary.

ABOVE Hose splitters (top left) and timers (top right) customize these spaghetti emitter drip systems. Flexible drip systems like these work well in container gardens, where the plastic nature of the drip line allows flexibility between different crop and container choices throughout the season.

Drip irrigation steadily feeds water onto the growing medium at the soil surface. The depth to which the soil is saturated depends in part upon the length of time, gallon-per-hour emission rate, and number of drip lines set up in any given bed or container. Drip irrigation can be used as point-to-point irrigation by using spaghetti emitters, like the one held above. The water carried through the lines drips out at a single point.

UP ON THE ROOF

The Gary Comer Youth Center

CHICAGO, ILLINOIS

Founded in 2009

Third-story green roof container garden

Total rooftop space: 8,600 square feet

Total planted space: 6,000 square feet

gcychome.org

In a protected rooftop courtyard three stories above the streets of Western Chicago, the Gary Comer Youth Center rooftop garden is a respite for neighborhood teenage green thumbs as well as for stopover visitors such as monarch butterflies and migratory birds. Although the landscape looks like a green roof, each row is actually a sunken container, fifty feet long and eighteen to twenty-four inches deep.

The roof was originally designed to use a sprinkler set up called a "riser system" with twelve-inch-, eighteen-inch-, and twenty-four-inch-high pop-up heads. Because of the wind and vegetation density, Garden Manager Marjorie Hess determined the system to be ineffective. Instead, she adapted a number of the pop-up heads to use with drip irrigation hoses on a timer system. Her advice? Remember that the roots of the plant are in the soil, and choose a watering system that most efficiently delivers water to the roots. While a sprinkler system might work well in some applications, for a garden of tall perennials and consistently spaced annual plants, drip irrigation works best.

Food from the Gary Comer Youth Center rooftop is used for a farmers' market that joins its produce to food crops grown at the Youth Center's neighboring ground–level site. Additionally, Hess provides space each year within the roof garden for teen program participants to experiment with their own crops.

*To be a
successful farmer
one must first
know the nature
of the soil.*

XENOPHON,
OECONOMICUS

The Dirt on Rooftop Soil

The narrative of your plants' success is going to be written in large part by the layer in which you plant their roots. Healthy soil is the keystone of all good plant production. In this chapter, we'll look at the characteristics of some of the growing mixes most frequently used on the rooftop. We'll assess how to measure their success, and how to amend the media with fertilizers suited for your growing site and plant needs. The last section of this chapter deals with composting, focusing on the best systems for a rooftop.

Growing media varies regionally in availability, cost, quality, and content. Do your research: your investment in the right media will write the future of your rooftop farm or garden.

Before we dig in, it's important to clarify what we mean by rooftop soil. Because I love soil so much, I will often catch myself referring to the green roof growing medium at the Eagle Street Rooftop Farm as "soil." Technically, "soil" is a naturally occurring substrate used in ground-level growing. Rooftops gardens and farms rarely use ground-level soil. Unaltered, these soils are too heavy. Instead, rooftop growers use manufactured mixes that address the same qualities of a good ground-level soil while honoring the concerns of weight load on a rooftop. These mixes are referred to as growing media. Green roof "soil" is a growing medium, as is potting soil. When choosing your growing medium, there are three qualities to look for: how well it holds and drains water, how well it retains nutrients and how much it weighs dry and saturated.

Green Roof Growing Media

Green roof growing media are specialized and often proprietary blends of organic and inorganic material. Because manufacturers are reluctant to reveal the proprietary components of their blends, you can instead ask for an analysis to ensure that the media meets the acknowledged standards of the FLL (The German Landscape Research, Development, and Construction Society). A good testing agency will offer an analysis that includes reference values that make the test results easy to read.

Most growing media are composed of 75 to 90 percent inorganic materials such as expanded shale or crushed clay and 25 to 10 percent humus, clean topsoil, or compost. Using aggregates bulks up the volume while reducing the weight of the medium. The materials used to create these blends varies regionally. Typical green roof media is not ideal for farming, as the mineral components may be too coarse, the organic matter content and nutrient levels likely too low, and the pH value is typically too high. As green roof farming gains popularity, growing medium manufacturers are doing good work researching how best to find the "sweet spot" blending rooftop soils appropriate for growing vegetable crops and edible perennials. Manufacturers are looking for low weight, good soil structure, higher than typical organic matter content, long-term structural stability, good water permeability, good water holding capacity, a neutral pH, and sufficient nutrients. Green roofs designed or modified to grow vegetable crops typically have a higher percentage of organic material (for example, compost, peat, bark, or coir) as part of their overall growing blend. For example, a typical green roof planted in drought-tolerant sedum would thrive at 10 percent organic material to 90 percent aggregate, by volume. But at the Eagle Street Rooftop Farm, the growing medium was blended at 40 percent organic material to 60 percent aggregate.

For a number of reasons, it's worth asking the company you're purchasing growing medium from what their blend is derived from. The compost could be made from wood products such as bark or wood chips, spent substrate from mushroom production, peat moss, or any number of other products. Compost blended into the medium should be well aged and free of weed seed and contaminants. Many agencies exist to check the quality of compost. For example, the United States Composting Council (USCC) website offers a regionally searchable listing of area compost supplies that meet its Seal of Testing Assurance (STA). Laurel Valley Soils, the local Mid-Atlantic compost source that manufactures Rooflite, the media manufacturer used by the Eagle Street Rooftop Farm, was recognized USCC Composter of the Year for 2013!

Container Soil

Container gardeners typically use potting soil as their growing media. Potting soils are soilless, instead using base ingredients of peat moss, perlite, and vermiculite. Each has characteristics that help with water retention, pore space (for water and airflow), and bulk up volume without adding much weight.

Common Components of Potting Mix

INGREDIENT	CHARACTERISTICS
Anything from animals (feathers, blood, manure)	Upcycled from animal processing, these various amendments generally add nitrogen to the mix. An alternative to blood meal and ground feathers is manure; bat and bird guano and chicken and cow manure are the most common. They should all be well-aged for your safety as well as to avoid causing nitrogen burn on your plant's roots. If making your own mix, wear gloves and a mouth and nose protector when adding these materials.
Anything from the sea with a shell (lobster, oyster)	These products vary by regional availability and are often sourced from the fishing industry. Shells are made of calcium, a necessary micronutrient for plants.
Coconut coir	Harvested from the outer husk of processed coconuts, coir is a fibrous product touted as a substitute for peat. Both dry are extremely light and compact, and saturated, can hold a good deal of water.
Compost	Compost is made from a wide range of materials, from vegetable scraps to sewage sludge. The detail-oriented rooftop gardener can call up the company in question and ask for their processing practices.
Forest loam or humus	Loam and humus are soils taken from land as it is cleared or developed. The terms apply to a crumbly, well-aggregated soil. Descriptors like "forest" can regionally indicate variation on acidity. A forest loam from the conifer-rich Pacific Northwest may very well have a lower pH than humus harvested from the prairie states. If you're feeling detail-oriented, check the origin of the product or call up the manufacturer and ask for the results of their pH test.

Additionally, potting soils will include a regional range of
additives designed to increase moisture-holding capacity
and fertility or balance the pH of the mix. These ingredients
are listed on the packaging. If you choose to use organic
potting mix blends (highly recommended), here are a
few good additives to look for and what they do for
your plants:

Common Components of Potting Mix

INGREDIENT	CHARACTERISTICS
Peat moss	Peat moss is derived from sphagnum moss, a genus of moss of which there are over a hundred species. In a potting mix, peat moss is frequently used as a base product to add volume while contributing little weight of its own. Peat moss can carry a significant amount of water, however, increasing the weight of your potting mix by up to twenty times its original weight. Over time, peat moss can dehydrate past recovery and will need to be amended with additional peat moss and other potting mix materials. Peat moss by its nature is slightly acidic.
Perlite	Frequently mistaken for fertilizer, the small, white, lightweight particulates of perlite are popped volcanic rock. They add air space to the soil, bulking up its volume while adding little weight. Perlite often migrates to the surface of the soil over time and can blow away. Work it back into the soil and amend as needed.
Vermiculite	Vermiculite's small, flaky, shiny particles are used in potting mix for plants and as a pure product for seed germination. It has the Goldilocks "just right" qualities of both breaking up sticky soils and being absorptive enough to retain and regulate moisture well.
Worm castings	Worm castings, typically harvested from commercial red wriggler vermicomposting operations, are nutrient-rich, pH balanced, and crumbly in texture. If you can find a mix with this amendment you will not only have a great soil product but also the happy possibility of introducing worms to your rooftop!

HOW TO CALCULATE THE SATURATED WEIGHT OF ADDITIONAL MEDIA

Particularly as vegetable growers and other extensive rooftop gardening fans clamor for an increase in organic matter content, stability is an important factor to take into account. The components that make up the organic matter content of a blend—including compost and potting mix basics such as peat, loam and humus—break down over time. This happens on the ground, in containers, and on green roofs. As the materials are weathered away or decompose naturally in the thriving landscape, the depth of the soil profile changes. Good gardeners usually amend this, as well as nutrient loss, by adding a topdressing of fresh organic matter. If this is your practice, you absolutely must determine whether the growing medium matches the weight load restrictions of the rooftop.

On a professional level calculating the saturated weight of media is done with compacted material and based on specific laboratory standards. For example, Penn State University offers to test media samples for saturated bulk density on a compression basis. If you're working with a structural engineer, this is the number they would ask for. For example, the bulk density (at maximum water capacity) of the media used at the Eagle Street Rooftop Farm (Rooflite Intensive Ag) is approximately seventy pounds per cubic foot, which is less than six pounds per square foot and inch. If you are well within the safe values of adding additional media, here's how you can do a basic analysis on your own: Find and weigh a container large enough to fit a square-foot sample of the medium. Put the medium in the container and submerge the medium in water for twenty-four hours. Then allow it to drain for fifteen minutes. Weigh the sample, subtracting the weight of the container. This is the weight of your saturated soil. You can continue to wait and weigh your medium to gauge its saturated weight at varying stages of saturation.

When first purchasing a green roof media, the weight of various soil media is provided by the manufacturer. A typical lightweight growing mix weighs about eight pounds per square foot, fully saturated at a one-inch depth. If you are raising your soil an additional three to four inches, be sure your roof can hold the additional twenty-plus pounds per square foot.

The Dirt on Peat Moss

Growing mixes are made from a wide range of ingredients, but most use peat moss as their base. Mosses are some of the oldest and simplest plants on earth, with an evolutionary history that dates back five hundred million years. They build stems, leaves, and reproductive structures, but not sophisticated conducting tissues, seeds, or flowers. We use one word—moss—to describe this simple plant. But there are in fact twenty-two thousand species of moss, of which sphagnum, the peat mosses, are a genus.

Sphagnum has a long history of human use as bandages, diapers, roofing and insulation materials, and most recently in horticulture as an ingredient in potting mix. When used as such, the twenty-plus species of sphagnum mosses are referred to as "peat" or "peat moss." To understand why peat moss is so useful to the gardener it helps to know how it functions botanically. Sphagnum are a bog plant. To survive, each plant keeps its "head" above water. The rest of the plant hangs below, saturated, trailing a tail of yards and yards of stem from which cluster thin leaves. Of these subaquatic leaves, only one in twenty cells are alive. The rest are dead cell walls and adept at one task only: absorbing water. The capacity to hold up to twenty times its weight in water is

BELOW, LEFT A moist pocket near a drain allows *Bryum argentum* moss to crop up, as well as a rare rooftop *Pila golfa*.

BELOW, RIGHT From left to right: peat moss, perlite, and vermiculite; pure compost; and peat moss with vermiculite.

what makes sphagnum so valuable to the horticulturalist. Additionally, when living, sphagnum naturally releases acids in order to access and absorb nutrients. Its low pH inhibits bacteria, giving sphagnum ideal antimicrobial and antifungal properties that engender it to a potting mix.

In a rooftop garden, the sight of moss outside of your potting mix is often cause for alarm. After all, the presence of moss signifies excessive moisture, anathema to a roof. I will add a silver lining to that cloud. As you remove the moss and solve your drainage issue, recognize that the presence of mosses also indicates the levels of minerals, heavy metals, and pH of what it grows on, be it your growing media or rooftop surface. Each species of moss is incredibly specific in the air pollution it can tolerate. For example, the penny-size domes of growth of *Ulota crispa* indicate that sulfur dioxide levels are below 0.004 ppm. *Bryum argenteum,* tenacious and easily recognized by its lamplight-like reproductive structure, is one of the more common urban mosses. You can learn a lot about your rooftop and the quality of life around your garden by learning more about your mosses.

Maintaining Healthy Soil

For some rooftop gardeners, focusing on soil health is like asking them to floss. We all know it's good for our health as a regular practice, but taking the extra step to do so takes a bit of discipline. Over time, your growing media are going to change. Before you end up with infertile, low-quality, compacted soil, incorporate a few regular practices. They're painless, I promise.

First, start with a good mix. If you are going to invest time, money, and research anywhere, focus on your growing medium. It will pay off in spades. Rather than replacing, you'll be able to amend, which over the long term is more affordable and better for your plants and soil biology.

Next, there are several basic cultural practices. Don't let moisture linger. Wet, poorly aerated growing medium

UP ON THE ROOF

AgroTech Paris

PARIS, FRANCE

Founded in 2012

Sixth-floor green roof container garden

Total rooftop space: 2,690 square feet

Total planted space: 1,614 square feet

From six stories up, the view from the AgroTech Metro rooftop garden in the Fifth Arrondissement neighborhood of Paris is postcard-perfect. The River Seine separates the Left Bank below the rooftop garden from its famous neighbor across the water, Notre Dame. The founders of this university-based experimental project were interested in blending a custom lightweight growing mix. For a drainage aggregate, instead of perlite they turned to pozzolana. This porous rock is the same material used in construction centuries ago when Paris's precursor, the bustling Gallic city of Lutetia, was built. Mixed with wood chips, the light, chambered rock is the perfect drainage material for the garden's raised beds. Additionally, the gardeners use local urban organic wastes: compost made from food and plant waste from Paris and Versailles, wood, coffee grounds, and *Pleurotus ostreatus* mycelium cropping residue from a nearby urban farm that produces these oyster mushrooms in shipping containers.

The growing media you use on your rooftop site will vary based on your geography.

UP ON THE ROOF

The Eagle Street Rooftop Farm

BROOKLYN, NEW YORK

Founded in 2009

Third-story green roof

Total rooftop space:
6,000 square feet

Total planted space:
5,420 square feet

RooftopFarms.org

At the Eagle Street Rooftop Farm, we employ two kinds of growing media. One is our primary medium, the green roof custom blend installed by Goode Green. This product was made by Rooflite, a Pennsylvania-based soil manufacturing company. For our containers, we use a lightweight potting mix blend manufactured by McEnroe Organic Farm in the Hudson Valley region of New York State. Although both products are lightweight, drain well, and use compost as part of their blend, they are different products from their origin story on up! To see the results, turn to the Introduction (page 1) for images of the farm.

At McEnroe Organic Farm in Millerton, New York, a bacteria-driven compost is made from a blend of organic matter such as compostable cutlery and plates, locally collected animal manure, and food scraps collected from various sources, including the nearby Culinary Institute of America (CIA).

At Laurel Valley Farms, Rooflite's Pennsylvania-based parent company, a fungi-driven compost is made from a blend of organic matter that includes ammonia–rich animal bedding and byproduct from the region's mushroom industry.

ACTNOMYETES

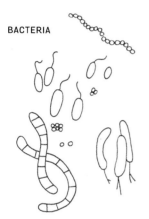

BACTERIA

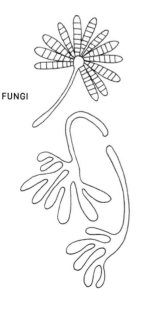

FUNGI

suffocates plant roots. A population of stinky denitrifying bacteria will boom: you'll smell them when you've got them! Wet growing medium promotes fungal diseases. If your potting mix is holding more water than usual, check if your containers are draining well. On a green roof, make sure all the drainage points are clean and clear at all times. If you are using a timer irrigation system, check that it's off when it's raining!

You should also address compaction regularly. Over time, container and green roof soils become compacted as the organic matter in their composition breaks down. Compaction collapses the pore spaces in soil, which can slowly destroy the air and water flow so vital for healthy microorganisms and plant roots. The best solution is to continuously work in compost if weight load allows, or to add (as needed) a lightweight drainage material such as clay particulates, perlite, peat moss, coconut coir, or vermiculite.

If it's a concern, test for and avoid contaminated soil. Heavy metal is a loosely used term to describe metallic elements of a few different classifications. The most notorious heavy metals are lead, mercury, cadmium, silver, and chromium. Even in small doses, they are toxic to people, animals, and plants. Because a rooftop is a designed growing environment, contaminated soil is rarely an issue. However, if the soil you've brought up is suspect, or over time you are concerned about atmospheric pollution building up in your soil, you can submit a sample for a heavy metals soil test at a private or cooperative extension laboratory.

Finally, you should pay attention to your soil food web. A teaspoon of healthy ground-level soil can host representatives of a hundred different species of nematodes, a thousand species of protozoa, twenty-five thousand species of fungi, seventy-five thousand species of bacteria, and a total population of one to seven billion organisms. These are small, small creatures. If bacteria were the size of the diameter of spaghetti, nematodes would be the size of a pencil's diameter, and protozoa the diameter of the circle your fingers make with the familiar U.S. gesture for "A-OK!" Soil mites and springtails would have the diameter of an average adult's arm span, while an average garden spider would be scaled up to the size of Michael Jordan's arm span (nearly seven feet, or two meters).

Plants have close relationships with each of these soil citizens. Until soil microbes render nutrients into a chemically accessible form for plants, the plants cannot use them. Nitrogen is the best example of this. Although the atmosphere is 78-percent nitrogen, plants cannot use it without the help of rhizobia (a specialized symbiotic bacteria that affiliates with every living plant—most famously with legumes—except those in the cole crop family). (Well, that is until the Haber-Bosch process for the manufacture of ammonia came along and changed agriculture forever. But that's a long story for another book.)

Another aspect of your soil food web to pay attention to is the larger guys: insects. Your soilless growing mix may start free of insects, but if you build it, they will come! The presence of visible insects is a good indicator of which smaller insects and microbes your growing medium hosts. Once you identify your insects, you can look up their diet and determine what smaller creatures or types of organic matter (your plants included) they like to eat.

Understanding Nutrient Availability

Plants access nutrients as ions dissolved in water. In ground-level soil, nutrients become available in the soil for plants as rocks (which are parent materials rich in minerals) weather, and as organic matter (anything that was once alive) is broken down by animals, insects, and microbes. In potting mixes and green roof media, manufacturers do their best to make mixes with these nutrients in an accessible form for plants. Two vital components of good soil structure are humus, or organic matter, and clay. These are adept at storing excess nutrients not yet used by plants. Here again, manufactured mixes make use of lightweight stand-ins for these vital soil components.

HOW TO BUILD A
BERLESE-TULLGREN FUNNEL

A century ago and a decade apart, an Italian entomologist (Antonio Berlese) and a Swedish zoologist (Albert Tullgren) created an incredibly simple tool for luring out and identifying ground-dwelling insects. I've used this technique on our green roof and was surprised by the diversity of insects living in our six-inch-deep green roof growing medium, particularly around our perennial plantings. A microscope helped me to identify even smaller creatures such as springtails (0.25 to six millimeters long!). Start with a small soil sample (for the size of jar listed here, a one cup sample will do). You'll get different results if you sample from the surface of the soil or deeper into your growing medium. Experiment, and see which critters you meet!

A desk lamp with a 25- to 40-watt lightbulb

A wide-mouthed 24-ounce glass jar

A 6-inch-square piece of black paper, curled into a funnel that fits inside the mouth of the jar

A slightly smaller piece of window screen

A small (for this size jar, ½ cup to 1 cup) sample of your growing media. I find that media samples from mulched areas, or sections of the rooftop planted with perennial plants or long-standing annuals yield the most interesting results!

Rubbing alcohol (to act as a preserving fluid)

1. Pour a small amount of rubbing alcohol (one to two inches should suffice) into the jar. Curl the black paper into a funnel and set in the mouth of the jar.

2. Place the window screen flat inside the funnel so it can hold the soil sample.

3. Place the soil sample on the screen.

4. Put the jar underneath the lamp or light source, with the light three inches above the sample. Over the course of two to five days, the insects in your soil sample will crawl away from the light source across the screen and fall into the rubbing alcohol.

Essential Soil Nutrients

Freely available nutrients	Carbon, hydrogen, oxygen	Basic component of all organic molecules: you, me, this book, plants. These three free and readily available nutrients make up approximately 95% of a plant.
Major macronutrients	Nitrogen, phosphorus, potassium	Collectively, these three are called the "major nutrients" or "macronutrients." On bags of fertilizer, nitrogen, phosphorus, and potassium are listed as N, P, and K respectively.
Additional macronutrients	Calcium, magnesium, sulfur	Calcium, magnesium, and sulfur are available in sufficient quantities in most soils. Potting mixes will frequently reference various materials (kelp meal, bone meal) that contribute to the available amounts of these macronutrients.
Micronutrients	Iron, boron, manganese, copper, zinc, molybdenum	If you routinely use compost or fertilizers like fish emulsion, you are likely supplying a sufficient replacement quantity of these micronutrients. If you use only amendments and fertilizers with macronutrients, over time you may see signs of micronutrient deficiency.
Even more micronutrients	Chlorine, nickel, cobalt, silicon	Plants cannot grow without these, but at such trace amounts it is not usually a concern for deficiency.

Cation exchange capacity. I'm a big fan of learning soil chemistry—it can be very useful when you're experiencing a problem you can't solve and are turning to some hard science to sort it out. Cation exchange capacity (CEC) is a good concept to start wrapping your head around both because it dramatically affects plant nutrition and because green roof growing media manufacturers love to talk about it.

Cation exchange capacity is the measure of your soil's ability to hold cations, or positively charged ions—for example, calcium (Ca_2+), magnesium (Mg_2+), sodium ($Na+$), and potassium ($K+$). In soils, clay and organic matter carry a negative surface charge. They are quite adept at attracting and retaining cations. Nutrients in the soil also present as anions, or negatively charged ions. This includes nitrogen ($N-$), phosphorus ($P-$), and sulfur ($S-$). During cold, wet times of year, when microbes are less active, growing medium is more prone to leaching anions.

One of the consequences of low cation exchange capacity in soil is that the pH will decrease with time, acidifying the growing medium. Lower pH inhibits proper nutrient uptake, no matter how much fertilizer you apply. I've found the best fix is to seasonally amend with organic matter to increase your media's CEC, typically a compost blended with the appropriate acid or alkaline granular amendment (such as lime or greensand) to adjust the pH of the media. Because the additional weight load can be problematic on a rooftop, I keep track of the saturated weights of the materials before topdressing.

Reusing Potting Soil

Every spring at the end of plant propagation season, and in the fall at the end of the container-garden growing year, rooftop gardeners wonder if they should throw out their soil. If possible, don't. This "tired" potting mix can be added to a compost pile or amended with fresh fertilizers such as compost or additional potting mix. If you're concerned about plant diseases, you can heat treat the soil between seasons. Use the soil chart that follows to determine the appropriate temperature, and use a soil thermometer to test your soil as it "bakes" to see if you've achieved the right heat. My preferred method of sterilizing potting soil is using solar energy. I spread all my potting soil out on a tarp, then cover it tightly with greenhouse plastic. Some growers with smaller quantities to solarize use glass or Plexiglass to bring up their soil temperature. I have also tried using an oven. This works best for small amounts of potting mix. Moisten the soil until it forms puddles when you press an imprint. Preheat the oven to 275°F. Most soil needs between 40 and 90 minutes. I warn you: this process smells incredibly strong, so be prepared! You can also use the microwave. Seven minutes in the microwave is fatal to most root-rot and damping-off fungi. Unfortunately, this method also seems to negatively affect soil pH, cation exchange capacity, and mineral content. This is not my preferred method. Nor is the technique—if it can be called that—of using boiling water. Pouring boiling water over potting soil will kill many, but not all, microorganisms, so it does not fully sterilize it.

Fatal Temperatures for Soil Pests and Pathogens

PESTS	30 MINUTES AT TEMPERATURE
Nematodes	120°F
Damping–off and soft–rot organisms	130°F
Most pathogenic bacteria and fungi	150°F
Soil insects and most plant virus	160°F
Most weed seeds	175°F
The remaining weed seeds and viruses	212°F

Testing Your Soil

When ground-level growers measure the success of their soil, they focus on its texture, pH, and available nutrients. The ratio of sand, silt, and clay in soil makes up its texture classification. Soil texture classification categorizes its drainage and compaction characteristics, or how well air and water move in your soil. Air and water movement influence the health of your soil's biology, or populations of insects and microbes. The pH of soil, which measures its acidity or alkalinity, is influenced by its composition and its microbe population. Plants have adapted to grow at an incredibly wide range of pH, but most of our vegetable crops are happiest between 6.3 and 7.0. Within this range, they (and the microbes that surround them) can access the nutrients they need to grow and thrive.

Rooftop growing medium is judged by a slightly different set of standards. For example, you can't take a traditional soil texture test, focusing on sand, silt, and clay, with green roof soil, a container potting mix, or a hydroponics system! To get to know your mix, start with these tests:

Soil pH. Soil pH is a measure of the concentration of hydrogen ions in a solution of soil and water. The pH scale is logarithmic, which makes the difference of a decimal have quite an impact. Soil with a pH of 6 is ten times more acidic than soil with a pH of 7, and soil with pH 7.2 is ten times less alkaline than soil with pH 8.2.

Most vegetables do best in soil that is slightly acidic, or pH 6.3 to 6.8. In this range, essential nutrients are more readily soluble and therefore more accessible to the plants. Part of their accessibility has to do with soil microorganisms, the most beneficial of which, for vegetables, are also happiest in this range. If the pH is too high or too low, the beneficial microorganism population begins to wane. Since it's the bacteria that make nutrients accessible, although a soil test may show plenty of nutrients, an improper pH won't let the plants have access to them. Purchasing a pH test kit is easy and using one even easier. You can test both your growing media and your water throughout the season, particularly as you start adding various amendments to your media.

Soil test with a cooperative extension. If you'd like to know more about the nutrients present in your growing medium, a soil test by your local land grant university cooperative extension will test both macro- and micronutrients, as well as toxins such as heavy metals. A laboratory soil test is recommended when you bring in new soil from unknown sources, as well as after a season or two of gardening when deciding what should be done to amend your beds. A good place to start is to test the pH; the basic levels of nitrogen, phosphorus, and potassium in the growing medium; and the micronutrients (calcium, magnesium, and so on). Most standard soil tests will at their most basic level additionally test what percentage of your soil is organic matter. Since your growing mix is manufactured, you probably know that information already. Once you have the test results back, call the laboratory. Particularly when working with extension agencies through a land grant university, the lab technicians are available to walk you through the results. Explain your unusual growing situation.

HOW TO INTRODUCE MYCORRHIZAL FUNGI TO YOUR GREEN ROOF

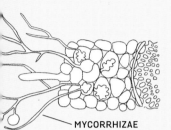

MYCORRHIZAE

Mycorrhizal fungi are one of the most fascinating, useful, and essential partners you'll have in maintaining a healthy rooftop garden. Fossils from 400 million years ago show plant roots encased with fungi. You're probably more familiar with these fungi than you think. For example, the familiar edible mushrooms chanterelles and *Boletus* are the fruiting bodies of two types of mycorrhizal mushrooms.

Most plants would far rather share nutrients to gain this fungal network than expend their resources growing plant roots. With the exception of plants in the Brassicacae family, most of the plants on earth (95 percent!) evolved a relationship with mycorrhizae. These fungi form symbiotic relationships with plant roots: the fungi receive sugars and amino acids from the plant, and the plant receives phosphates and other nutrients. Endomycorrhizae are the more common group of mycorrhizae likely associated with your rooftop crops. Endomycorrhizae use their hyphae to penetrate the cell walls (but not the cell membrane) of plant roots. The hyphae then branch out within the cell, increasing their absorptive surface area. In the meantime, fine threads of connected mycorrhizae extend from that original anchor out into the soil. These fungi are also particularly good at reaching into the smaller pore spaces in soil, which draws up even more moisture to their plant hosts.

There are two tricks to introduce mycorrhizal populations to your rooftop. One is to purchase a commercial inoculant. These are readily available online. Confirm that the mycorrhizae you've purchased are the right ones for your plants. They will arrive dehydrated, with application instructions to wet and distribute them in your growing medium. Another trick is to simply scoop up soil from a healthy site growing similar species of crops and mix it with your growing media. That said, a scoop is all-inclusive, so you'll get millions of other microbes as well—good and bad.

Fertilizing: What Works, What Doesn't, and Why

In your first year of rooftop gardening, your growing medium may be rich enough to sustain healthy growth. Over time, however, the nutrients in your growing medium will diminish as they either leach out or are used up by your plants. Rooftop gardeners and farmers can address this nutrient loss by using fertilizers. There are many types of fertilizers and many ways to apply them. Here, we'll take a broad view of the basics: what it means to use organic and synthetic fertilizers, applying fertilizers as liquids versus granular delivery, and when and how to apply fertilizers throughout the growing season. Fertilizers, when purchased as packaged products, come with clear instructions that should be followed exactly. We'll not repeat them here.

Organic and Synthetic Fertilizers

Fertilizers deliver nutrients to the soil. Soil biology delivers nutrients to plants. I use organic fertilizers for a range of reasons, but the most important is for the health of my plants. If you feed your plant with synthetic fertilizers, they will spend less of their energy producing the root exudates that encourage their symbiotic relationship with soil microbes. Over time, while feeding your plants, you're decreasing the population of your soil biology.

Organic fertilizers are derived from material that used to be alive. Organic fertilizers use a wide range of base products to provide the nutrients you're looking for, as well as many macronutrients. Contrast this with synthetic fertilizers, which are manufactured and delivered mainly in the form of salts. As the salts dissolve in water, the salt itself stays in the soil, while the nutrients are drawn up by your plants. Because synthetic fertilizers dissolve so readily, they tend to be fast-acting. Plants will absorb these easily accessible, simple nutrients at the expense of other nutrients. Soil scientists call this "luxury consumption." For example, when a plant is overfed nitrogen, it accumulates in the plant's tissues as nitrates rather than protein nitrogen. Excess nitrates crowd out the plant's ability to process nitrogen into proteins, because the nitrates replace the micronutrients essential to the amino acid conversion process: iron, copper, and molybdenum. Excess phosphorus suppresses zinc, copper, and iron uptake, and excess potassium in a plant's tissues will prevent the uptake of calcium and magnesium.

A final problem with regular use of synthetic fertilizers (there are more, but this one's worth mentioning here) is salt buildup. You'll notice salt buildup as white residue around the lip of your rooftop container right above the soil line, or on the surface of the growing medium. It can also cause browning of the plant's leaf tips. To get rid of excess salts, flush water through the container for several minutes, then allow the soil to dry out. Continue to water heavily until the salt residue stops reappearing. Unfortunately, this practice also drains nutrients from the soil.

Liquid and Granular Fertilizers

Most liquid fertilizers are sold as concentrates. These are diluted before you use them to water the plants. It's best to use liquid fertilizers early in the day. When the sun is strongest in the middle of the day, any residual fertilizer can burn your plant's leaves.

Granular fertilizers are sold as manufactured pellets, or as a raw material in a chalky or sandy form. These are applied in small amounts around the plant (a practice referred to as sidedressing), or worked into the soil before planting. Take care not to put these directly near the plant's roots, as this can "burn" them. No matter which product you choose, you should wear gloves and avoid inhaling it as you apply it.

If you're using a packaged fertilizer, take a look at two things: the nutrients they contain and in what form, and the rate of application. Follow the recommended rate of application precisely! Unfortunately, excessive fertilizing is an incredibly common practice both on the roof and on the ground. It does your plants no good and can in fact damage them, even when using an organic product.

When to Apply Fertilizer

Many plants and plant families are heavy feeders that may require additional compost or fertilizer throughout the season. This second boost should be a low-nitrogen fertilizer. Fertilizers are often labeled for their nitrogen-potassium-phosphorus ratio, or NPK. These numbers are listed in order on the product's label. In this instance, look for a 5-10-10, 6-8-8, or 5-10-5.

Examples of in-season light to moderate applications of fertilizer include:

- Topdressing, such as an application of compost approximately one inch deep across the surface area of the container or the entire bed.

- Sidedressing, such as applying a granular, organic nitrogen source like soy or alfalfa meal, one to two tablespoons around each plant, scratched in lightly.

- Foliar feeding, such as a weekly or bimonthly application of heavily diluted foliar fertilizers, including compost tea, liquid seaweed, and fish emulsion, as directed by product label.

Managing fertilizer throughout the season is a practice best established according to your plants' needs, your growing medium, and your local weather. For example, at the Eagle Street Rooftop Farm, we grow salad greens and peppers regularly every season. We have cold, wet springs and hot, dry summers. I avoid using liquid fertilizers in the wet spring, when it will run off easily; I watch the weather to make best use of the product I choose. Generally, we amend our soil twice yearly: once in the spring before planting, with a topdressing of an inch of compost across all the green roof row beds, and once during transplant season for our chiles, typically in May, with an organic slow-release granular fertilizer product mostly (to our staff's amusement) made of bird or bat guano. The salad greens, whose leafy growth benefits from a nitrogen-rich fertilizer, are given liquid applications of fertilizer approximately two weeks after germination and a minimum of a week before being harvested. That way they are not too young to be fertilized nor too close to harvest so as to taste of the fish emulsion, compost tea, or whichever organic product we happen to have used. We apply the same liquid fertilizer to our chiles until they set flowers, at which point we stop feeding them nitrogen-rich fertilizers, which would encourage leaf growth over flower and fruit set. Around late August, while the chiles are fruiting, we start to sow cover crop in the empty beds and around existing plantings, to get it established before the frost in late October. We use legume cover crops like vetch and clover, inoculated with mycorrhizae by soaking the seeds overnight with a bit of the dehydrated bacteria (it looks like black chalk dust). If the year of composting has gone well, we'll topdress with compost once more in the late summer, but not in the late fall. We often leave our compost soil in the bins over the winter, so all our decomposers have a safe haven and plenty to eat during the cold months of the year. The most valuable amendments to our compost pile include animal manure, generously donated by our egg-laying hens, who live on the roof in a twenty-five-foot-long covered run with a coop on one end, and our rabbits, who live downstairs in our market room, coming up for outings in a pop-up rabbit pen when it's not too hot. The qualities of the manures vary—chicken manure is much harsher on our plants than rabbit droppings— and both are required to be well-aged before they go near any food crops. As we clean the animals' coop and cages, respectively, we collect the bedding and manure as one, turning it out into our compost bins to the delight of the microbes within. Their population explodes, our food and plant waste breaks down faster, and with no trips downstairs needed, we produce a rooftop-ready product that feeds our soil.

Rooftop Composting

Rather than carrying plant material from pruned perennial and pulled annual plants downstairs to put in the trash, composting is a straightforward way to close the loop on the nutrients withdrawn from your growing medium by each cycle of annual vegetables. Even adding rooftop-safe small amounts of finished compost can help maintain good drainage, airflow, and organic matter content in your original growing medium.

Before you start composting, check whether it is legal in your city's building and fire code. Many cities deem an open-air compost system (such as a bin system) a fire hazard, while permitting closed-bin systems (such as a tumbler).

There are many different styles of composting: free-standing systems like piles and windrows, enclosed simple machines like tumblers, and prescribed techniques like lasagna composting or the Bokashi method. Most traditional composting systems operate best at a one-cubic-yard size. At that volume, the core of the pile can reach the temperature and moisture levels needed to host the bacteria specific to the decomposition cycle of nitrogen-rich waste like food scraps and fresh plant material.

Don't put a compost system on your rooftop if your rooftop can't hold its weight. While some rooftops can support a one-cubic-yard compost pile (Eagle Street Rooftop Farm, for example, has a three-bin system on a section of the rooftop with good line load capacity), many cannot. Plant material—especially food waste—adds up as you add it little by little.

Don't compost using a system that leaks excess moisture in a way that could damage the rooftop membrane.

Composting allows the grower to see food through its full cycle, from field to fork—then reinvested back into your rooftop.

Open-bottom systems are an absolute no-no. This is a classic system on the ground, but it does not suit a rooftop. Instead, most of the rooftop gardens and farms featured in this book use tumblers, Bokashi bins, screened bottom bins, forced air composting, and modified container-based composting to keep their compost clean and tidy. Here we'll look at those methods and ways to troubleshoot some of the issues inherent in closed-bin composting (such as tumblers).

At first glance, composting can seem like an overwhelming task. Don't be intimidated. Composting is like cooking. You can start with a recipe, but develop your own style appropriate to the site, resources and time. It's worth it. Compost is a free, rich source of nutrients. If you want to grow healthy plants, you have to have healthy soil. The future of gardening and farming is written in how we treat our soil, and that includes rooftops.

How Compost Works

Compost is the finished soil product made from decomposed organic matter. Compost happens because you create an environment hospitable to decomposers in your compost pile. The range of visible and microscopic decomposers is incredibly vast. Each is specialized to thrive at a certain range of temperature and moisture level, and each enjoys a particular diet. As you get to know the insects and microbes in your compost system by their preferences and functions, making a compost pile starts to feel like throwing a party. You put together the right food (organic matter) and atmosphere (temperature and moisture levels), and the guests start arriving. If they are having a good time, they stick around and invite all their friends. As they enjoy themselves—you get compost!

So how to best host a party for invisible guests? Turning organic matter into compost soil relies on the right temperature, moisture, and airflow. In a typical decomposition cycle, this cast of characters is divided as primary, secondary, and tertiary decomposers for the order in which they eat and excrete organic matter, turning it into compost soil. Physical decomposers like worms, fly and beetle larvae, ants and others grind, bite, tear, chew, and suck materials into smaller pieces

GROW WITH THE PROS

Orren Fox

AUTHOR OF HEALTHY, HAPPY CHICKENS

Happychickens
layhealthyeggs
.blogspot.com

ORPINGTON

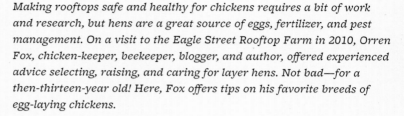

Making rooftops safe and healthy for chickens requires a bit of work and research, but hens are a great source of eggs, fertilizer, and pest management. On a visit to the Eagle Street Rooftop Farm in 2010, Orren Fox, chicken-keeper, beekeeper, blogger, and author, offered experienced advice selecting, raising, and caring for layer hens. Not bad—for a then-thirteen-year old! Here, Fox offers tips on his favorite breeds of egg-laying chickens.

Orpington. Big, friendly, and very adaptable to all weather, Orpingtons are good layers, have great personalities, and are very low-maintenance.

Brahama. Brahama are a fancy breed of chicken with the feathers all about their feet (which requires a bit of care, especially in the winter). They add a certain style to your flock while being very cold-tolerant, super social, but just okay layers. Bantam Brahmas are like balls of feathers and the sweetest birds.

Cochin. Cochins are not very good layers but they are absolutely beautiful. They have full feathers all the way down their legs and feet.

Rhode Island Red. These are no-fuss birds. Rhode Island Reds are often considered aloof but very inquisitive. This is a great breed to guarantee high egg yield from the flock.

Leghorn. When kids draw or think of chickens this is that chicken. They are not quite as hardy in cold temperatures due to their large comb. The White Leghorn is thought to be an amazing egg layer (especially in the low light of winter) but also considered a bit standoffish.

BRAHAMA

COCHIN

RHODE ISLAND RED

LEGHORN

using a wide range of fascinatingly diverse and complex mouth and digestive systems. The many decomposers you can't see (without a microscope) are the rooftop-friendly fungi, actino- mycetes, and bacteria. They are lightweight, fast at what they do, and easily and invisibly predominant in a rooftop system.

By nature of their remove, rooftops don't always host the same familiar primary decomposers as ground-level com- post systems. When you add to your pile a large amount of pruned branches from your rooftop raspberries, for example, the woody-tissue-eating primary decomposers simply may not be there to eat it. It will take additional time, moisture, and heat to get the smaller secondary and tertiary decom- posers on the job. At that stage, the material is more pliant and palatable.

Choosing a Composting System

Compost systems are often classified as "hot" or "cold" sys- tems. Hot piles are actively managed. You add materials and turn and aerate the pile. Cold piles are passively managed, usually by layering materials and letting them sit to decom- pose over time. If food waste isn't breaking down quickly enough, cold composting can attract animal pests. Cold com- post heavy with carbon-rich materials can be a fire hazard.

Bin composting. Bin systems work well staged as a three-bin system. Typically, one bin is reserved for active loading of compostable materials, a holding bin for carbon-rich browns and nitrogen-rich greens. Keeping it divided between the two is helpful for the second stage. The second bin hosts a pile in the process of decomposition to which browns and greens, chopped small, are added. The final bin holds a resting pile no longer receiving browns and greens. Eventually, this bin contains the finished compost, ready to be sifted and used. Traditional bin systems (at a cubic yard in capacity or larger) can be heavier than what many rooftops can bear. The best bin systems are placed on point-loading sections of the rooftop, are kept moist during drier periods of the year, and are actively managed to encourage quick decomposition and deter pests.

UP ON THE ROOF

The Windy City Harvest Rooftop Farm

McCORMICK PLACE, CHICAGO, ILLINOIS

Founded in 2013

Fifth-story green roof container garden

Total rooftop space: 30,000 square feet

Total planted space: 22,000 square feet

ChicagoBotanic.org

Preexisting green roofs can serve as a great springboard for sky-high vegetable growing, but swapping sedum for squash requires restorative care. Five stories up above the hot concrete streets of the Near South Side neighborhood of Chicago, the Chicago Botanical Garden's Windy City Growers annexed a nearly three-acre green roof on the McCormick Convention Center and converted twenty-two thousand square feet from green roof sedum to vegetables. The preexisting growing mix was composed of composite shale, sand, and organic matter at a depth of approximately four inches. After consulting with a structural engineer, the Windy City Growers added a three-inch topdressing of compost, vermicompost, and granular fertilizer.

The head farmer, Darius Jones, noticed that around the edges of the bed where the soil was higher, plants thrived. Instead of topdressing the entire rooftop by laying down additional growing media, the farmers now employ innovative techniques like selectively mounding the soil around the plants, and using landscaping fabric-built bags to create small, deeper pockets for some of the long-term plants like chiles and tomatoes. This system accommodates the plants' needs with little impact on the overall weight load of the growing system on the rooftop.

LEFT, TOP AND BOTTOM
The western side shows the
"before" of the McCormick Center
green roof while the rooftop's
eastern side shows the dramatic
"after" and future possibilities.

TOP, RIGHT Windy City staff
harvest produce for an in-house
catering company.

Tumbler system. Tumblers are closed-system compost bins (usually barrels) on a mount or with a crank that allows them to be turned (tumbled). They are tidy, animal-proof, and don't leach, which is good for both the rooftop and the compost quality. Tumblers work best when the materials added are finely chopped. If you produce a significant amount of plant material, consider multiple tumblers. Tumblers perform best when not overloaded, as the crank can break.

Upright barrel/trash can system. A compromise between a bin system and a tumbler, these closed systems are praised as tidy and animal-proof. They work for both hot and cold composting. You must allow for airflow and drainage, via holes, or these systems quickly become anaerobic as the organic matter breaks down. Protect your roof by placing a saucer or other form of water catchment below the system.

Forced air system. The forced air compost system is widely used as a speedy, efficient way to promote good airflow and the correct temperature for bacteria to thrive in a compost pile. Perforated pipes running through the compost pile are fed air via an external blower, such that no part of the pile is more than eighteen inches from an air source. The blower operates on a timer, pushing air through the pile, generally for three to four minutes every twenty minutes or so. A forced air system works best on a rooftop that can bear the weight. Forced air composting systems function best at a large size (three by three by three, or twenty-seven cubic feet). Whether running off of a solar-powered motor or the building's grid, they require electricity.

Bokashi composting. The Bokashi method of composting, in which compostable materials are tightly packed into a sealed container, is an anaerobic compost system. Aerobic compost piles have lots of oxygen; anaerobic piles do not. Anaerobic compost tends to smell sulfuric or putrid, thanks to the bacteria it hosts and the acids these bacteria excrete. Many rooftop gardeners turn to Bokashi to quickly break down organic matter. In a Bokashi system, specific anaerobic microbes with less intense-smelling excretions are selected

The compost system you use is based on local law, weight constraints, and how much organic matter you're hoping to compost. From top: The bin system at Eagle Street Rooftop Farm in Brooklyn, New York; a closed tumbler system at Noble Rot in Portland, Oregon, and a close look at the empty interior of a newly built forced air compost system at Stone Barns Center for Food and Agriculture.

to inoculate your bucket of organic matter. Fed a little sugar (typically, barley or molasses is suggested), the bacteria population booms, and your organic matter quickly starts to decompose at the mercy of their ravenous appetites.

Although using the Bokashi method can save you the space of building a three-bin system or save you from the smells of compost-ready food waste while it builds up in your apartment or home, it is important to recognize that Bokashi does not create finished compost. The decomposing organic matter created by Bokashi composting must be added to another compost pile or a fallow area of your rooftop site to further break down.

Best Practices for Composting

Different compost systems produce different results. The best systems for rooftops take into account weight load and safe drainage. No matter what system you choose, here's what you need to keep an eye on:

Materials added. Everything breaks down, but the balance of "browns" and "greens" your pile holds will determine how well and how quickly this happens. Piles heavy in greens—nitrogen-rich food waste—need less additional moisture and more additional turning and aeration. Piles heavy in carbon-rich dried plant material—browns—need more supplementary watering and attention to the size of the material being added. One of the easiest ways to tell if you are adding enough of both is not by weight or volume (see the carbon-to-nitrogen section that follows) but by the smell of the pile. As it processes, hot, funky, and slightly sweet is best. Typically, too many nitrogen-rich materials lead to a putrid, sour, sulfuric smell, which can indicate too much moisture and too little air. Generally, too many carbon-rich materials generate no smell at all—a sign that compost isn't happening!

The size of the materials added. Small is beautiful! Chopping compostable materials down to one to three inches in size helps speed up the work your decomposers are doing.

The temperature of the core of the pile. As the different decomposer populations take their turn in breaking down the organic matter in your pile, the core of the compost will rise in temperature. As the organic matter is broken down and becomes compost, the temperature will lower again. The bacteria most effective at composting thrive at a temperature between 140°F to 160°F. If your pile does not reach that temperature, a different population of decomposers will dominate the process of breaking down the organic matter. It will happen, but more slowly.

Airflow in the pile. Your active aeration of the pile (turning, tumbling, forced air) promotes the population of oxygen-loving aerobic bacteria. When a pile becomes compacted or waterlogged, anaerobic bacteria that thrive without oxygen take over. Anaerobic bacteria can quickly putrefy your compost. They excrete sulfur compounds and change the pH of finished compost. On the other hand, too much air in your compost pile can keep temperatures too cool to host either bacteria population and can slow the compost process down.

Moisture levels in the pile. Almost everything that lives in a healthy, active compost pile enjoys some moisture to move and reproduce. Too much moisture disrupts airflow. Too little is a fire hazard. The microorganisms in a compost pile are generally happiest at 50-percent moisture. Most compost with food waste and other nitrogen-rich "greens" will have sufficient moisture levels. If not, water the pile. Some closed compost systems (tumblers, for example) have problems with too much moisture. If that's the case, ease up on the nitrogen-rich materials until you can rebalance your pile.

The Ingredients of Composting: Browns and Greens

Compost experts often use the term "carbon-to-nitrogen ratio" to describe how they balance "browns" and "greens" in their pile. For example, vegetable waste has a carbon-to-nitrogen ratio of 12:1 or 25:1 depending on how fresh or dry it is when

NITROGEN/PROTEIN RICH ("GREENS")

- Cover crops, as well as peas, beans, and other legumes
- Crushed eggshells
- Sour milk
- Human hair
- Coffee grounds
- Fresh animal manure and bedding
- Kitchen scraps

CARBON–RICH ("BROWNS")

- Dry grass clippings, leaves, straw and hay
- Sawdust, wood shavings
- Newspaper
- Dry plant material
- Rice or cocoa hulls
- Aged animal manure and bedding

used. Fruit waste has a carbon-to-nitrogen ratio of 35:1. An ideal pile would balance out between 25:1 and 30:1. If you can't be bothered to figure out the ratio of everything you put into your pile, just know that nitrogen-rich materials tend to be fresher, wetter, and softer; carbon-rich materials tend toward older, dryer, and stronger or tougher. The labels "greens" and "browns" can be misleading—coffee grounds, for example, are brown in color but a "green" in the compost pile.

While all organic matter breaks down, some materials should be added to a compost pile with a degree of caution. If you're composting with human hair, sawdust, newspaper, weedy plant material, aged manure, sod, grass clippings, or any other material that might have questionable chemicals in it, feel free to politely ask your source if they know anything about its origins, use, and treatment. It's not just your safety, but the health of the billions of organisms in your compost pile that is affected by the various materials used. Manures, sod, and weeds all can contain seeds, which in a cooler-temperature pile (or if they are weed seeds, which are *tough!*) will cause you no end of problems if imported through the compost you cheerfully use to topdress the following year. Be equally cautious if composting plant material with fungal or bacterial disease pathogens. While temperatures above 140°F can kill off many pathogens and weed seeds, at temperatures above 160°F the pile runs the risk of becoming sterile. Because rooftop compost systems tend to be smaller than ground-level bins, compost with care bread, grains, fats, oils, grease, meat scraps, bones, and cheese. They are slower to break down and can attract unwanted insects and animals. If you do chose to compost them, make sure the pile is well-maintained and hot. Add them to the core of the pile, not on top.

Troubleshooting

Making compost is an art and science. Practice and observation—two handy life skills—are particularly useful when troubleshooting composting problems (see the chart, opposite). Don't despair. Remind yourself: compost happens!

Compost Troubleshooting

PROBLEM	LIKELY CAUSE	FIX IT BY . . .
Pile appears and feels dry; doesn't heat up	Too dry	Add more nitrogenous materials. Add water until core of pile feels evenly moist. In dry periods of the year, check this regularly. In dry climates, covering the pile with a tarp helps retain moisture. If you do tarp your pile on a rooftop, affix or weight down the tarp.
Pile doesn't heat up; feels moist	Pile is too small	An ideal pile is 1 cubic yard, or approximately 3 by 3 by 3 feet. Smaller piles tend to cold-compost, never reaching the higher temperatures a bacterially active pile will. This simply means the compost will take longer. Because the temperatures stay low, this style of pile will also not kill many diseases or weed seeds.
Large pile, not hot, feels moist	Not enough nitrogen materials	Add nitrogen-rich materials and turn the pile.
Pile cools off before most material has fully decomposed	Needs aeration	Turn the pile using a compost corkscrew and/or garden fork, mixing the center material with outer (and less-composted) materials.
Pile smells bad, looks and feels wet	Too much moisture	Add dry, carbon-rich materials, and turn the pile. In rainy periods of the year or rainy climates, use a tarp to cover the pile.
All the material not breaking down	Too dry or not enough nitrogen	Add water until the center of the pile is evenly moist; cover with a tarp to retain water. Add nitrogen-rich materials and turn the pile.
Matted layers, not breaking down	Needs to be mixed	Turn pile, and chop large material into 3- to 6-inch-long pieces.

HOW TO BUILD A WORM BIN

Worm composting, or vermicomposting, is a smart and efficient way to produce a fine, nutrient-rich material to amend your rooftop garden's growing medium or to use to topdress your farm site. Worm bins can be designed as indoor or outdoor systems. Outdoors, the worms must be kept in a cool, shady place. While the bacteria in a compost bin thrive at temperatures from 130°F to 160°F, worms bins do best in temperatures familiar from ground-level soil, a much cooler 50°F to 80°F. In four-season climates where the temperature drops below freezing, your worms will go dormant in a cluster at the core of the bin. Moving into the fall, stop harvesting castings from the worm bin to ensure they have enough bedding inside the bin to burrow into for the winter. Wrap the bin in an insulating material and a waterproof layer to prevent it from freezing. Ideally, come springtime, overwintered worm eggs will hatch to replace any lost population of adult worms.

Two 14-gallon plastic bins with lids

A drill with a ¼- to ⅜-inch drill bit

Several pieces of thick cardboard or wood

A piece of fine mesh window screen at least 1 foot by 1 foot

8 ounces sterile sand

Three issues' worth soy-based ink newspaper or equivalent corrugated cardboard

Permanent marker

Duct tape

One spray bottle with water

2 cups old-fashioned rolled oats

Red wiggler worms, ideally at least 1 pound

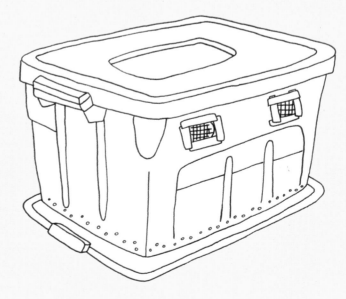

1. Lay one of the bins on its side on top of the wood or cardboard. Using the permanent marker, make three to six marks around the sides of the container, an inch above the bottom of the bin. These are your drainage holes. Drill them out, using the wood or cardboard to protect the surface under the bin from being punctured by the drill bit.

2. Within six inches from the top of the bin, draw two three-inch-diameter circles, two on each long side of the bin. Again using the wood or cardboard to protect the surface under the bin, use the drill the outline their circumference. Pop out the circles.

3. Cut the window screen into pieces large enough to generously cover each of the drainage holes and upper portholes. Use the duct tape to affix the screen to the bin. (While aesthetically this looks better taped on the inside, if taped on the outside, it's easier to repair and replace.)

4. Shred the newspaper into one-inch strips lengthwise. Add to the bin in light, fluffy layers, misting gently with water. Continue until the bin is three-quarters full of news-paper. Add the sand, and toss to coat the moist newspaper.

5. Open up a small pocket in the middle of the newspaper and add the worms. Fold the newspaper back over them gently. Add the oats in a single clump at the top of the pile. Moisten the oats, then cover with a fine layer of newspaper and close the bin.

6. Use the second bin's lid as a saucer for your worm bin. Prep the second bin as you did this one to prepare it to be a replacement bin, or keep as-is and use to double-insulate your worm bin in the wintertime.

7. You can start feeding the worms small amounts of food waste as soon as the starter material of oatmeal is gone. The larger the worm population, the more food waste you can add.

8. After a few months, as the worms work their way through the food scraps, you'll see less bedding and more compost appear in your bin. Stop adding food scraps to the bin for two weeks. Then gently push the bin's contents to one side of the bin. Put fresh bedding in the empty half, and in the following 2–3 weeks, add food waste only to the freshly prepared half. In that time, the worms will migrate to that side of the bin. Remove the compost, sift, and return any unbroken-down material to the worm bin.

*Each of us might aspire
to be a connoisseur
of nature, and
connoisseurship implies
a combination of
knowledge on one hand
and love on the other.*

COLIN TUDGE

5

Rooftop Seeds and Starts

Faced now with the blank canvas of rooftop site and
growing medium, it's time to start planting! In this
chapter we'll look at best practices for seed-starting and
purchasing transplants (plant starts). This information
should be just enough to whet your appetite to learn
more, make better use of your time and money, and
address some of the most frequently asked questions
for successfully starting plants on a rooftop.

I'm often asked what grows best on a rooftop. Start by selecting plants that you love to eat, smell, and look at, and enjoy working with. You'll put more time and research into taking care of something you are already excited about. I know that I spring out of bed at six in the morning to check in on my rooftop-grown chiles because I am passionate about peppers. After identifying what you like to grow, work within its plant family, varieties of the same species, or plants with similar growing characteristics to find a few that will work on your roof. All you need to do is fulfill the golden rule of good growing: "Match the right plant to the right place." Chapter 2 can help you make these decisions. Plants thrive when you strike the right notes to create a harmonious chord of their climate preferences (temperature, light, precipitation), the growing medium you use (quality, depth, available nutrients), and the choices you make as you grow them.

At first glance it looks like a lot to keep track of, but don't worry. Try something new, fail, and figure out why. Ignorance is *not* bliss: it is disempowerment. Hone your sense of curiosity, adventure, stewardship, and observation. Plants that failed to survive and thrive in one round can perk up in a different microclimate or through another season of better seasonal weather. Try different cultural care and disease and pest control. Experiment with your growing medium or choice of plant cultivar.

How Plants Work

Before you start growing, a basic understanding of plant structure and function can help determine what will grow well on your roof. As students we are taught to identify plants as a six-part object (root, stem, leaves, flowers, fruits, and seeds) that rely on three things to grow (light, air, and water). To many of us, plants remain robotic, simplistic living things that perform photosynthesis, reproduce, and thrive or thwart us as they silently proceed through their life cycle. Alas, that so many of us leave it at that! Plants are tremendously varied and dynamic.

This superficial summary should serve as a springboard toward learning more. You'll find yourself to be a stronger green thumb on your rooftop for understanding how plants work.

Roots

Roots are no mere anchor! Roots are the diplomats to the bustling world of mineral nutrients, water, and oxygen below the surface of your growing medium. The microscopic area of the soil surrounding each root and root hair, the rhizosphere, is like a busy lunch counter. Plants proffer sugars and other exudates to the bacteria and fungi that sidle up for a meal. In return, these microorganisms engage in a healthy elbows-out battle to maintain their place at the trough. They render mineral elements in the soil accessible to plants, and many protect the roots from disease pathogens.

Taproots develop best in full-sun, well-irrigated conditions.

The rooftop gardener should know three things about roots. First, for our edible plant choices, the total mass of a plant's roots is equal to its size. For a large plant (that big, bushy, indeterminate tomato), you need a large volume container—deep or wide. Second, the more root hairs, the more water and nutrients a plant can absorb. If you pull a plant out of your growing medium and the roots rip freely rather than clinging to the soil, the plant's roots weren't very healthy. Perfect your watering practices to encourage long, deep root systems within the confines of the container system or green roof and make sure your growing medium is giving your plants what they need. Third, the partnership between roots and microorganisms is an important one. Many rooftop growers use inoculants (typically dehydrated microorganisms) to kick-start life in their soil. Read up on the right product and practices for your plants. You can learn more about mycorrizal fungi on page 105.

Stems

The higher plants (our herbaceous and woody stemmed edibles and ornamentals) use their stem to conduct water, minerals, and nutrients between the leaves and the roots.

Opuntia grows easily on a rooftop. Its leaves are modified into prickly, drought-tolerant spines, and its stem is a water-holding, photosynthesizing, paddle-shaped structure. Its fruit is one of many types of edible prickly pear.

For most plants, the main stem, or stalk, holds the plant's leaves away from its neighbors and keeps the plant upright. There are a few aspects of stems to pay attention to on a rooftop. This is particularly true for the rooftop gardener interested in space-saving vertical growing. Stems can climb (such as peas), creep (such as watermelon), cane (like bamboo), or spread underground as a rhizome (like ginger). On top of that, not all vertical climbing stems climb, creep, or spread in the same way. Some grasp with tendrils, others stick to a surface with "hairs," and still others use suckers to climb.

Leaves

The rooftop gardener can approach leaf crops with three strategies in mind. First, even in the most extreme growing circumstances (high and lows of wind, temperature, light), a plant will still grow leaves. Keep this in mind when choosing your crop list: a failing crop of spinach, kale, or basil is edible, whereas a fruitless crop of tomatoes has only inedible leaves to show for your labor. Second, even a broad-strokes understanding of leaves' adaptations to heat and drought can help narrow down a plant palette on a difficult rooftop. Plants with reduced leaves such as those on succulents, leathery leaves, waxy cuticles, hairy leaves, and a reduced number of stoma on their leaves are all great candidates for a hot, dry rooftop. Next time you're wandering through a plant nursery, keep your eyes peeled and your fingers reaching for waxy, fuzzy, prickly plants. Finally, keep in mind the life cycle of your plant palette's leaves. Dry, shedding leaves can be a fire hazard on a roof, or block your drainage system. Be prepared to provide the care when your leaves start to litter.

Rooftop fruit can range from tomatoes to peaches.

Flowers, Fruits, and Seeds

For plants, the production of flowers, fruits, and seeds typically comes after putting a good deal of investment and energy into roots, stems, and leaves. Flower, fruit, and seed crops take effort! Growing fruiting plants (such as zucchini, tomatoes) requires plenty of sunlight, water, and nutrients to pull off a bumper crop. Rooftop growers should be aware, too, of how their plants pollinate. On the other hand, under duress, leaf crops (basil, lettuce) and taproots (radishes) can become bitter or more sharply flavored as they draw sugars from their leaves to put forth flowers. Rooftop growers should be aware, too, of how their plants pollinate. Some (tomatoes) self-pollinate, and fruit will result with only one plant present. Others (squash) require a pollinator to move pollen from the male to female flower on a single plant or multiple plants. Still others (corn) are wind pollinated and do best planted in a block rather than planted alone. For the rooftop with dioecious plants, which have male and female members, if you're planting a sole specimen make sure that a neighborhood plant is nearby, on the roof or at ground level, to cross-pollinate with. It would be a shame to bring a sweet cherry tree all the way up to the roof and have it fail to bear fruit, waxing lonesome for lack of a dance partner each spring.

Growing from Seeds

Starting your rooftop garden from seed and taking it all the way to harvest is a real pleasure. With seeds, you will have access to not only a wider range of interesting plants to grow than you'll find with commercially available starts, but also a broader range of varieties of each type of plant. Growing from seeds is a little bit of extra work, but significantly less expensive than starting your entire rooftop garden from transplants. You can even grow from seed for free if you save seeds yourself from plants you've cultivated or trade seeds with other seed savers. As you spend more time gardening, learning your rooftop site, and talking to other gardeners, you'll find you can actively seek out seeds that are known to do well, thanks to the testimony of fellow green thumbs. If you happen to visit a friend's rooftop garden and see a plant you think does well, or if you visit a ground-level garden or farm and admire the health and productivity of their crops, ask where they got their seeds. Take into account their spacing practices, growing mix, watering regime, and microclimate.

Starting Seeds on the Rooftop and Indoors

Rooftop gardeners have a few options for seed-starting. Seeds can be started indoors in a well-lit room or under plant lights, or in a propagation space like a greenhouse. Starting seeds indoors is useful for getting your plants started early before the rooftop outdoor growing season has begun. At transplant size, your plants will need to be hardened off— that is, acclimated to the rooftop growing environment. If you grow in a four-season climate but want to maximize the yield you get in your slightly shorter growing season, start plants in the nightshade family (eggplants, peppers, tomatoes) early and indoors. Fruit (and seeds) are the last thing those plants make in their growing cycle, so if you can jump-start leaf, root, and stem production, you're that much closer to the part of the plant you want to eat!

Seeds can also be started outdoors. For this method, you'll need to keep an eye on the weather. The temperature of your potting mix or growing medium typically has to be above 68°F for vegetable seeds to germinate successfully. As with indoor seed-starting, you can sow seeds outdoors in plant flats or pots, then transplant them to give them more room to grow. Be aware that on a rooftop, wind and sun can dehydrate shallow plant flats quickly. Another method is to treat a deeper, larger container as a plant nursery. Sow the seeds thickly, as you would in a plant flat. From this close planting, transplant them out into the proper spacing, following the timing you would if they were in a plant flat. For periods of the year with regular rainfall, this works beautifully for growing rooftop-acclimatized crops.

Certain seeds are known to benefit from direct sowing. These plants don't handle transplanting well, usually because of a specialized root structure (like a taproot, such as carrots and plants in the carrot family: dill, cilantro, etc.). Legumes (peas, beans, and soybeans) tend to direct sow better than transplant. These seeds should be planted where you would ultimately like them to grow. To ensure a good germination rate, you can overplant, then thin the seedlings.

The distance between the plant light and plants profoundly affects their growth! Keeping lights two to three inches above the plant at seedling stage will prevent them from having weak, over-lengthened stems.

Guides like planting frames help with uniform results. Here, rooftop–ready seedlings are closely sown, then later transplanted further apart on the rooftop.

Whether starting seeds indoor or outdoors, focus on:

Containers. Use any container that can hold two to four inches of potting soil. The container must provide for drainage and airflow. Plant flats and other containers of uniform size make watering and plant care easier.

Soil. Start seeds in a potting mix. These are lightweight and sterile and allow good drainage while holding moisture well. Before planting, moisten the potting mix in a clean container with warm water until it clumps but does not lose water when squeezed.

Temperature. Most garden seeds (especially vegetable seeds) need a soil temperature of 70°F to 75°F to germinate. Their preferences are often indicated on their seed packet. Keep soil warm on a mat or near a radiator; avoid windowsills (or cover with a newspaper at night). Seedlings do well with air temperature between 60°F-70°F.

Water. Most seeds need moisture to germinate. To prevent desiccation on a rooftop, you can use a plant flat with a clear plastic hood (tape it to the flat, so it won't blow away!), or adapt your container using tented plastic or a floating row cover like Reemay. When seedlings sprout, balance watering thoroughly to encourage deep root growth with allowing the potting soil to dry out slightly between watering, to prevent compaction and root rot.

Fertilizer. This is optional. If your soilless mixture does not contain compost or organic fertilizers, use an organic liquid fertilizer as soon as seedlings have robust, true leaves or after they have been stepped up to larger container. It's vital to dilute the fertilizer (half strength at the maximum!). An application every week to ten days is plenty often.

Light. Most vegetable seeds do not require light to germinate; some flowers do. Plant these seeds on the surface of your potting soil. As soon as the seedling emerges, provide a direct light source. Light is extremely important for seedlings. Lack of light makes seedlings leggy and weak-stemmed. They will transplant poorly, especially when exposed to rooftop sun and wind for the first time. If you are starting your rooftop crops indoors, use south-facing windows if possible, and rotate seedlings to prevent them from reaching and bending toward the light source. Rearrange plants once a week so that all plants get the same amount of light.

Artificial light sources should be placed as directly above the seedlings as possible (fluorescents, for example, are hung every one-by-four-foot growing area). The light source should be no more than two to three inches above the tallest part of the plant. As they grow, raise the lights. Lights can be on for twelve to sixteen hours a day. A daily period of darkness (and rest!) is important for plants.

Depending on the bulb type you use, you'll have to replace your lights on a schedule or your plants won't get the range of light they need to thrive. For some fluorescent lights, for example, replacement is recommended every six months. When researching the cost of each, keep the replacement factor in mind, and find the appropriate recycling facility for your bulbs.

In addition to lights, many growers also use a timer. Plants need a period of darkness of about eight hours per light cycle, and a timer can help establish a healthy cycle between the two.

These tomato plants were started from seed on the same date. The larger plant was stepped up to a larger container two weeks after it germinated. The smaller tomato plant was never stepped up. Three weeks later, this photo was taken. Who wore it best?

HOW TO BUILD A COLD FRAME

Cold frames are easy-to-move, low-maintenance mini greenhouses. Before you build your cold frame, determine if your local building code permits its construction and use on your rooftop.

Cold frames are designed to trap sunlight through a clear plastic, glass, or fiberglass sash. On the ground, cold frames can be framed out using straw bales, concrete, or stone. On a rooftop, wood or bespoke metal framing is preferable, as both are easy to customize and durable. The length of your cold frame depends on your site and available sash material. The width should be no more than thirty to thirty-six inches so that it's easy to reach across. Position your cold frame facing south for maximum sun exposure.

WOOD, FOR THE LID

Three 72" 1 by 2s

Three 34½" 1 by 2s

Three 33" 1 by 2s

WOOD, FOR THE BASE

Four 31½" 2 by 6s

Five 71" 2 by 6s

One 33" 2 by 6, the length cut diagonally to make two equal pieces

Two 9½" 2 by 2s

Two 15" 2 by 2s

HARDWARE

One 72" by 36" sheet clear acrylic

Three 3" stainless steel or brass strap hinges

Twenty-four 1¼" stainless steel self-tapping decking screws

Forty-six 3" stainless steel self-tapping decking screws

Fourteen ¾" stainless steel pan-head screws

Optional: one solar-operated vent opener. A wax-filled piston will open the cold frame lid on sunny days to prevent overheating. Charleysgreenhouse.com carries a good one (model No. 3515).

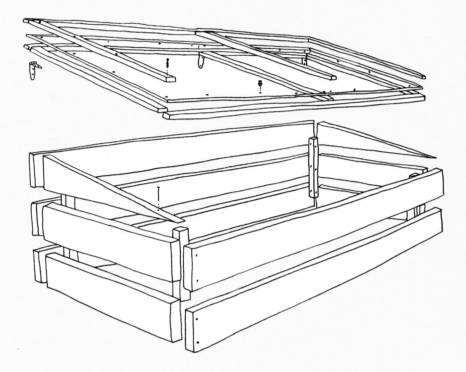

Predrill all your holes to prevent the wood from splitting and the acrylic from cracking.

1. Screw two of the 71″ boards into the butt ends of two of the 31½″ boards to make a shallow box. Attach the 2 by 2s in each corner to provide the framework for the next layer of 71″ and 31½″ boards. Screw on a second set of 71″ by 31½″ boards. For the top layer of the frame, screw on the diagonally cut 33″ 2 by 6 boards and the final 71″ 2 by 6s.

2. To assemble the lid, clamp the acrylic sheet between the 1 by 2s. Use 1¼″ decking screws spaced about 12 inches apart to attach the layers. Three sections (top, sides) of the lid need two pieces (sandwiching the acrylic). No strip is needed on the bottom; this allows the snow and rain to drain more easily. On this front piece, use the pan-head screws to fasten the acrylic to the wood.

3. Use the 3″ strap hinges to affix the lid to the cold frame. If desired, open the cold frame lid and install the solar-operated vent opener according to the manufacturer's instructions.

Plant Lights for Seedlings

BULB TYPE	WHAT YOU NEED TO KNOW
Incandescent	Readily available. Emits about 10% as light and the rest as heat. Use with caution: can "cook" seedlings. Not commonly used for plant starts.
Fluorescent	Least expensive option. Emits two to three times more light than incandescent bulbs. Readily available. Lifespan of 16,000 to 20,000 hours. Look for T12 magnetic or more efficient electronic bulb. Look for "natural light spectrum" models.
Full-Spectrum Fluorescent	Top choice of year-round growers. Lifespan of 24,000 hours. Look for T8 and T5 bulbs.
High-Intensity Discharge (HID)	More expensive but twice as efficient as fluorescents. Available as red/orange "MH" bulbs and blue/green "HPS" bulbs. Good directly for plant growth; terrible for the ambiance of a room.
Light-Emitting Diode (LED)	More expensive than fluorescents. Most commonly used in commercial propagation and greenhouse conditions.

If your seeds don't come up, start troubleshooting. Is the seed nonviable? Is the soil temperature outside its ideal range? Did you overwater or let the seeds dry out? To ensure that I have something to show for my efforts, I'll sow repeats of the same seeds five to ten days apart. That way I don't have to wait the full days-to-germination period to find out if they're good or not. Once the seeds start coming up, I stop repeat sowing.

Purchasing Rooftop-Ready Seeds

You can buy seeds directly from a brick-and-mortar store or order directly from seed catalogues (that's what I do). Seed catalogues are produced by companies that aggregate seeds saved from plants selected and grown out by seed savers and plant breeders. Because of the unique growing challenges of a rooftop, it is both fun and advantageous to have such a wide selection of plants to choose from. You can look for the seeds of plants described as having qualities like heat-tolerance or dwarf growing habit, and for varieties unusual enough to make all those trips up and down the stairs worthwhile. If you call up seed breeders and ask for their advice, they are rarely reticent about sharing lessons learned and favorite plants with you. (Favorite seed companies are listed in the Resources, page 239.)

Although plant nerds and farmers have swapped seeds for millennia, commercial seed catalogues and seed packets are a relatively new gambit in the grand scheme of agriculture, dating back to the eighteenth century. From the start, they have been well designed and hyperbolic in their promises of offering the most prolific, tallest, juiciest, most robust vegetable you could possibly grow. But they are also chockablock full of useful information. Here's what you should home in on:

- *The common name of the plant and its botanical name.* The botanical name, given in Latin, will help identify what plant family your seeds belong to. This will help with crop rotation, as well as grouping rooftop-ready plants for their shared characteristics by family. Common names are shared by some plants; the Latin name helps differentiate them.

- *Seed-sowing instructions.* The seed packet will include information about the ideal soil temperature for successful germination, the depth at which to plant the seeds, the spacing between the seeds, and the expected days to germination. It may also include particular tips for germination (say, whether it requires light, a period of dormancy, or scarification to germinate).

Seed packets vary in design. Pictures are pretty, but look for brass tacks information that will help you get growing.

- *Transplant and planting information.* This includes information about preferred habitat (sun or shade, soil type and pH, or cold-weather tolerance), and advice for spacing the seeds or transplants on your rooftop. Spacing, in particular, is a guideline, not a rule. Many rooftop growers use intensive or square-foot gardening methods to get more seeds and transplants into a smaller space.

Some companies will also include:

- *Cultural notes.* This could include flavor, productivity, disease-tolerance, and historical information and antidotes.

- *Care over time.* Your care of the plant will include thinning, transplant timing, pest and disease management, fertility management, seed-saving techniques, and much more. Seed packets will often include a few pieces of advice on these points. I take them fairly seriously: the packet doesn't have a lot of real estate to make comments, so if they've included it, it's worth paying attention to at least once.

You should always:

· Reseal the packet, keep the seeds dry, and follow storage instructions (generally a cool, dry place). Don't forget that inside those seeds are live plants. Within the seed coat—the hard, dry skin of the seed—is everything a plant needs to grow: the starter food of the cotyledon, and the complete plant embryo of root, shoot, and first leaf or leaves. Temperature fluctuation and moisture can trigger the germination process.

· If not indicated on the packet already, write the year you ordered the seed on the seed packet in permanent marker.

As you can see in the chart below, many seeds (kept in good condition) will stay viable for many years. These are extremely conservative numbers—a suggestion as to when you should start testing, not tossing. For crops not listed here, including herbs and flowers, you can use the information on the seed packet to tell you the expected days to germination.

Seed Viability and Germination Rates

ESTIMATED NUMBER OF YEARS THE SEEDS ARE VIABLE	CROPS, LISTED WITH EXPECTED DAYS TO GERMINATION
One year	Onion (10–14)
Two years	Corn (7–10), pepper (10–14)
Three years	Bean (7–10), carrot (12–15), pea (7–14)
Four years	Beet (7–14), eggplant (10–12), kale (5–10), squash (7–14), Swiss chard (7–14), tomato (7–14), turnip (7–14)
Five years	Broccoli (5–10), cabbage (5–10), cauliflower (5–10), cucumber (7–10), lettuce (7–10), melon (5–10), radish (5–7), spinach (7–14)

Seeds to Transplant

After a short time in a plant flat, seedlings thrive when moved from small seed-starting flats to larger transplant pots. This gives you the opportunity to vet your seedlings. As you step up, or transplant, your seedlings, examine the plants. Choose the strongest, fastest growers to step up. Stepping up plants stimulates new root growth as old growth is gently tickled (or more roughly torn). The plant leaves will benefit, too: more space will allow for better airflow between plants.

Hardening off. The hardening-off process transitions indoor or greenhouse plants to the outdoor setting. Hardening off seedlings allows them to adjust to cooler nighttime temperatures, significantly more light, and what's likely to be a dramatic increase in wind on the rooftop.

Cold frames are used to harden off plants, acclimating tender growth to the great big rooftop world.

Depending on the space and structures you have available to you and what is permitted on your rooftop space, hardening off can take place in a more gradual fashion by using structures like cold frames and shade nurseries. If you don't have the roof space or weight-bearing capacity to harden plants off in a structure, aim to put them in a shadier and wind-sheltered part of the roof their first days out in the sun. Think ahead when you're planting your seedlings in their pots, and use containers that are easy to cluster. For example, using a single plant flat instead of fifteen recycled plastic yogurt containers can make it much easier to take one trip up the stairs.

After their first few days outside, if your plants look pale, shrivel up, or fall over, they probably have the plant version of sunburn. Examine their newest leaves to see how green and healthy they look. If the new leaves are fine, there's a chance the plant will bounce back and adapt to the new environment. Often a mature plant with healthy roots will simply suffer the setback of sun- and windburn by shedding the old leaves grown in the lower-light space and putting forth new leaves adapted to the new source. Just keep an eye on them and make sure they have enough water and shade!

HOW TO START SEEDS IN GROUND AND IN FLATS

Seeds can be direct sown, or started in plant flats and then transplanted. Here are a few of my favorite methods and the reasons and timing for each.

Top, right. Sowing seeds outdoors, nursery-style. Typically, once your growing media is at or warmer than 68°F, you can sow seeds outdoors. Here, we use an empty rooftop container to sow seeds close together as though planting them in a plant flat. After they germinate and develop their first true leaves (at about two to three inches tall), the seedlings are transplanted out to the distance the mature plant requires. This technique is similar to the French Intensive method described by Bill Shores on page 174. At the Eagle Street Rooftop Farm, we use this technique weekly during the middle of the growing season to start succession plantings of our fall harvest crops, including kale, chard, fall lettuces, short-season tomatoes, cucumbers, winter and summer squash, and annual herbs. Since we are up on the roof taking care of our mature crops anyway, this technique saves us space and time (Chapter Seven has more details).

Middle, right. Direct-sowing seeds. While waiting for other plants to mature, we direct-sow seeds below our established crops. This is partially a companion planting technique (you can learn more about companion planting in Chapter Eight). It's also financially smart. Here, while waiting for pepper plants to fruit, we plant quick-to-yield crops like radishes and microgreens (mustards, lettuces). They're harvested by the time we are picking peppers.

Bottom, right. Growing plants in flats. Plant flats yield plant plugs, or small, uniform seedlings for transplant. They are typically used indoors to start seedlings early in the growing season before outdoor temperatures warm up. This is particularly useful for plants that require a long growing season when you live in a short growing season zone. For example, some of my favorite chili plants take 90 full days to grow fruit, and will continue to fruit for a month after that. To give them a head start, I sow the seeds indoors in plant flats before I transplant them outside. Seedlings in plant flats perform best when given the right light and a chance to harden off before going outside. You can read more about starting seeds indoors on pages 130–136.

HOW TO TEST GERMINATION RATES

If you have seeds left over at the end of your growing season, keep them. When kept in good condition, seeds can remain viable for quite a long time—indeed, some remain viable for years. If you can test the germination rates of your seeds a few weeks before your growing season starts, you'll know how many new replacement packets you have to order. It's up to you if you plant seeds with a low germination rate or compost them. I plant mine, doubling or tripling the number of seeds in each planting space to account for their low success rate.

A small plastic sandwich bag per seed type

One paper towel per seed type

A permanent marker

Water

1. Select ten seeds per seed packet. Write the name of the seed variety, the company name, the date, and the days to germination on the plastic sandwich bag.

2. Wet the paper towel, then squeeze out the water until just moist.

3. Fold the moist paper towel so that it fits inside the bag.

4. Place the seeds inside the paper towel. Keep the paper towel moist (similar to potting soil).

5. Keep the bag in the light exposure and temperature range required by the seeds inside. For example, to test the germination rate of peppers, keep the bag in a warm (above 70°F) place. Depending on the temperature, you may have to rewet the paper towel.

6. Within the days-to-germination range, look for sprouts. If a week after the last expected germination date the seeds have not come up, count those that have sprouted. To calculate percentage of germination, multiply times ten. For example, if three pepper seeds of the ten have sprouted, your packet has a germination success rate of 30 percent.

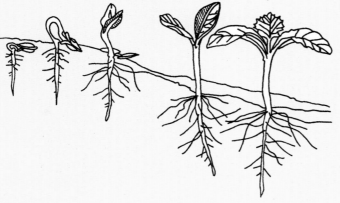

Transplants and Plant Starts

For rooftop growers without the right space to start seeds (or looking for instant satisfaction), plant starts or transplants are the way to go.

Smart Shopping for Transplants

Not all plant starts are created equal. When purchasing transplants, here are a few qualities to keep an eye on:

Purchase the plant for its roots, stems, and leaves. Because they look beautiful and sell better when flowering or fruiting, transplants are often sold at that stage. But if the plant's flowering energies are spent at the nursery, it won't perform as well when trying to root up and leaf out on your roof. Rather than getting the sneak preview, seek out the plant that hasn't flowered yet. Look it up by name to see what its flowers will look like in a few weeks when it's growing strong

The Eagle Street Rooftop Farm works with a rural greenhouse grower, Evolutionary Organics, to start warm-season transplants.

on your roof. As long as your transplant has unopened buds, pinch off the open flowers after transplanting. The remaining buds will bloom once the plant is established.

While at the nursery, flip the plant pot over gently and look at the drainage holes in the bottom. As plants sit waiting to be sold, they can become root-bound. Root-bound plants have packed, cramped swirls of roots at the bottom of their container. Look for plants with roots the right size for the container they're sold in.

Small is beautiful. The smaller your transplants are when you purchase them, the healthier and more well-adjusted they'll be on your rooftop. At a smaller size and younger age, the transition to a different temperature, wind, and growing medium blend will be less of a rude shock. Transplanting smaller plants also gives you the space around the transplants to direct sow seeds or intercrop with more transplants. As you harvest, you'll make room for your transplants to continue to grow.

Don't bring along uninvited guests. Before purchasing a transplant, check the plant thoroughly for insect pests and evidence of diseases caused by bacteria and fungi. Don't pay for something that brings along unwanted guests! Look for uneven coloration, leaf margin and leaf tip damage, obvious bite marks, systemic wilting (a sign of potential root problems), and of course, insects. Many pest insects like to hang out on the underside of leaves along the midrib. Feel free to ask the plant nursery staff to help identify the problems. Ask if they are cultural (local to the nursery site) and easily outgrown, or something you'll be carrying with you when you go. If you are absolutely wedded to purchasing the transplant but it does seem to have some faults, definitely inquire what remedies they would recommend. Sometimes it's as simple as removing the damaged leaves and letting the plant grow back in a healthy state on your rooftop.

Pick what you want, not just what you see. Particularly for long-term plants like perennials and trees, it's worth being choosy about the variety you want to grow. Educate yourself about what grows well on your site, and you can select for better cultivars. If the big-box store near you only has three kinds of apple trees, don't stop (or start!) there. Consider the potential of the fifty-year friendship that will evolve between you and your trees, and cast a wider net for a greater range of choices. If you are willing to start with a smaller plant, be it an annual or a perennial, you'll often end up with a wider range of cultivars and more affordable options.

Go for the pros. The closer you get to the person who actually bred, raised, and cared for the plants, the more information you'll have about your transplant. A good plant nursery staff will not only be able to give you growing tips for the next few months of care for your plant, but may also have tips to help you with the challenges of your unique growing space. If I'm going to spend money on plants, I'd like the two cents of advice as a bonus.

Rooftop-Ready Seed Saving

As plants prove themselves in the unique growing environment of your rooftop, it's worth saving their seeds to capture the developing strengths of each variety. Follow these tips to do so successfully:

Allow the plant you'd like to seed save to set seeds. If you're growing a crop for its root, stem, leaf, or fruit, you may eat it all year without ever seeing its seed. Kale, for example, can only be seed saved if you allow it to flower and set seeds. Earlier in the season, I'll tie a ribbon or put a planting label next to the plants that seem to be performing well. This will remind me not to harvest or pull them before they have a chance to set seeds.

Select for and save the seeds of the strongest performing plants on your rooftop to promote rooftop-ready traits.

Consider how the plant pollinates. If you'd like to save seeds from a plant that self-pollinates, no problem: the seeds you save should stay true to type. If a plant cross-pollinates with another variety of the same plant (for example, squash), the seed you save will be a hybrid—and the plant you grow the following season may have some surprise characteristics! Remember, most individual plants are going to produce hundreds to thousands of seeds. Figuring out how to isolate them during pollination is not as onerous as it sounds! An easy way to isolate plants is to time your planting so that the two varieties aren't flowering at the same time. Many seed savers use pollination barriers such as a light row cover cloth or caging while the plant is setting pollen.

Start with a seed that breeds true. It's easiest to start by saving the seeds of plants that were originally open-pollinated (OP) varieties (this includes heirlooms as a subset). OP and heirloom seeds will grow "true to type," meaning the seeds you save will not revert back to unwanted surprise qualities, as they would if you seed saved a hybrid. For example, Sungold F1 cherry tomatoes are a favorite hybrid of ours to grow on the rooftop. Every year a few fruit self-sow (fall on the ground, rot, and sprout seeds). The resulting tomatoes are cherry tomatoes, but often red! This is because Sungold, as the F1 indicates, is a cross of two different parent plants. Rather than seed save from our Sungolds, I save the seeds of our cherry type tomatoes that are true to type. That way, I know what I'm getting when I plant the following year.

Save the seeds according to the best practices for that crop. Carrots, kale, and calendula all have different seed saving needs; so do tomatoes and cucumbers. Generally, collect the seeds when they appear fully mature (often this means dry). Separate the seed from any remaining flower or fruit plant parts and store it in a cool, dry place.

GROW WITH THE PROS

Ken Greene

FOUNDER,
HUDSON VALLEY
SEED LIBRARY

SeedLibrary.org

Selectively seed-saving keeps the culture in agriculture. Here, heirloom advocate and seed-saving expert Ken Greene shares his tips for how—and why—to get started.

My motto is: "No seeds, no food. Know seeds, know food." Even if you don't plan on growing plants to save seeds on a commercial scale, becoming a seed saver will help you understand the plants you grow on a deeper level. You'll experience the full life cycle of the plants and gain a new appreciation for them as living beings. For example, we don't usually eat lettuce past its leaves, but it makes beautiful flowers and seeds when left to bolt. Sadly, despite such a long shared history between plants and people, this inherited cultural and genetic legacy is in danger of being lost. Even though the rooftop is considered a new and growing field, we have a lot of translatable skills from agriculture's past to raise to the roof.

It's unfortunate that most seed companies carry the same or very similar seed stock, bred for generic qualities like uniformity, shelf life, and ease of mechanical harvesting and shipping. If you want amazing flavors, colors, textures, shapes, and regional adaptations, stick to heirlooms and open-pollinated varieties. Each time you grow seeds from an heirloom strain you are growing its full history. You can grow a story about labs, white coats, genetically engineered technology, cheap labor, and poisonous ecological practices—or you can grow seed stories with flavor, travel, humor, intrigue, history, fair farm labor, and organic integrity.

Rooftop gardens and farms face challenges like growing with too much sun, shade, or heat; compromised soil health, wind, disease, and pest pressure. Brassicas like kale and mustards, microgreen mixes, and hearty Mediterranean culinary herbs do well in rooftop conditions. Space-saving climbing crops like peas, beans, and cucumbers can be trellised to make excellent use of limited rooftop space. There is a definite need for flowers. Many growers overlook flowers if they are not interested in them as a commodity crop. But cities need habitat for pollinators and other beneficial insects. Many flowers can do double duty as cut flowers for sale and natural habitat. Consider growing some native flowering species. Growing medicinal herbs can help us care for our communities in new ways. Plants are resilient and surprising. Seeking out and choosing new varieties with every new season is part of the adventure!

There are trees of a thousand kinds and all with their own exquisite kinds of fruits and all smell so that it is a marvel. I am the most sorrowful man in the world, not being acquainted with them.

CHRISTOPHER COLUMBUS,
UPON ARRIVING IN
CUBA IN 1492

Flowers, Herbs, Shrubs, and Trees

When advocates tout the benefits of rooftop gardening as a part of a landscape that retains stormwater, mitigates heat island effect, and provides pollinator habitat, much of that data is derived from green roofs landscaped with perennial plants. Flowers, herbs, shrubs, and trees are strong candidates for the perennial rooftop landscape. Strawberries and sage, peach trees and mint, grape vines and agave are all examples of edible and rooftop-ready plants that will come back strong year after year given the right growing conditions.

Select and plant your perennials with their mature size and growth habit in mind. This includes size, color, and points of interest like flowers, but also what the plant will look like throughout the year. The winter silhouette of a bare fruit tree is a very different profile in a container than a berry bush that gets cut back to the base of the stem every fall.

Cross-Compare Perennial Plant Needs

PERENNIAL FRUIT	IDEAL PH	IDEAL GROWING MEDIA CONDITIONS	LONG-TERM CARE
Blackberry	5.0–6.0	Well-drained, rich	Thorny! Mulch well around the base of the shrub, or you'll be weeding in a prickly place.
Blueberry	4.0–5.5	Moist but well-drained	Known to be shallow-rooted. Mulch with materials that tend toward acidity, such as chopped oak leaves or pine needles. Requires more regular nitrogen fertilizing than other fruits.
Cranberry and lingonberry	4.2–5.0	Very moist, rich	Bog plants. These favor soil rich in peat moss or acidic bark mulch.
Grape	5.5–7.0	Tolerant of any type, as long as it's well-drained	Deep roots. Rich soil and overfertilization can lead to poorly flavored grapes.
Red raspberry and black raspberry	5.5–7.0 and 5.0–6.5	Well-drained, rich	Both produce suckers, or lower growth, that need to be pruned if sprawling growth is not desired. Be aware of potential cross-pathogen issues between black raspberries and red raspberries, and avoid planting susceptible varieties on the same site.
Rhubarb	5.5–7.0	Tolerant of any type, as long as it's rich	Heavy feeder that does well with a midsummer and fall topdressing.
Strawberry	5.0–6.5	Well-drained	Unlike other perennials, should not be fertilized in the spring unless specifically recommended to that variety, or soft berries will result.

Propagating and Purchasing Perennials

Perennials can be grown from seed, raised from transplants, or started from a cutting. Some perennial plants have super-specific needs for seeding. This could include scarification, sun or heat exposure, or a period of chilled dormancy before they'll germinate successfully. Likewise, the technique of taking a cutting is specific to the plant. For example, strawberries can be grown from seed or by rooting up a portion of their stem where nodes with root tissue-producing cells reside. Woody stemmed plants like herbs, shrubs, and trees can be cut for sections of stem with dormant buds and promoted to root up with the right conditions of moisture, temperature, and a touch of rooting hormone. Keep in mind that a cutting is a genetic clone of the parent plant, and select the plant whose every quality you like before snipping off your new plant start.

Start your perennials in a space or container that will accommodate a season or a couple of seasons of growth. Too large a container runs the risk of getting waterlogged, and it's

LEFT Planting fruit–bearing shrubs is a low–profile way to establish edible fruit crops that don't need half the space or a fifth of the weight of a tree crop.

RIGHT If a certain perennial suits your roof, explore all the varieties available. Here, sage and a variegated sage thrive.

Woody-stemmed plants such as herbs, trees, and shrubs are easily propagated by taking a cutting.

a waste of unused nutrients and rooftop weight to have soil fill where a plant's new roots can't reach. Keep the roots in check to protect your roof membrane. If you're planting perennials known for their spreading growth habit, such as mint or raspberries, consider growing them in a confined space.

Perennials need seasonal care. Cutting back, pruning, and deadheading perennials is part of what keeps them healthy and attractive. If you don't want to have an unsightly fire hazard or drain-clogging plant debris problem on your rooftop, research the best practices for keeping your plant in good shape, and the best place to put your plant waste.

When you initially plant your perennials, do so according to their soil preferences. Drainage, pH, and organic matter content are all characteristics to look at before putting perennial plants together in a container or in the same growing media on a green roof. For example, plants like blueberries and strawberries taste good together in a fruit salad, but they grow in very different soils! A few examples of the variation between popular edible perennials are listed on page 150.

Growing Herbs

Herbs are plants with culinary, medicinal, dyeing, or decorative uses; for their potency of scent and flavor, they are used in small quantities. What a gift they are to the rooftop gardener, for no matter how slowly they grow or how picky they may seem about having just the right conditions, their small but aromatic presence is large!

Many herbs used well together in the kitchen have different needs while growing. A familiarity with plant families helps organize herbs by their nutrient needs, irrigation preferences, and growth habit. Additionally, while some herbs are hearty enough to overwinter as perennials, others are too tender to make it past frost. The growth habit of herbs is also important. Slow growers should be planted separately from spreaders, which will quickly out-compete them and steal their space.

SPACE–TIME PLANTING: ANNUAL AND PERENNIAL HERBS

In the first year, plant chives to the side, basil in the middle, and oregano on the other side. In the fall, pull the annual basil, and prune down the chives and oregano to overwinter them. In the second year, dig out and split the chives, transplanting half to a new container and repotting half in the original container. Replant basil. Allow the oregano to grow back. In the third year, the chives and oregano will have annexed most of the container. At this point, it is your choice to continue to divide and spread out the chives and oregano to allow both to thrive, or remove one and allow the remaining herb to take over the container. The steps outlined in this example can be applied to most combinations of annual and perennial herbs.

As an example, we can use three popular herbs in one hypothetical 1 foot by 1½ foot growing space as shown above. All three of these taste delicious on pizza, but have different care requirements over time.

Growing Rooftop Flowers

Flowers transform a landscape with color, form, and motion. The breadth of rooftop-ready flowers is incredible. To focus your choices, consider your goals. Are you growing flowers to improve the look of a landscape? Think about the mature size, bloom time, and seasonal habit of the plant, not just the flower. Do you want color all year long? Look at the bloom times of various plants, and orchestrate your rooftop to pass notes of color from one spot to the next as each grouping of plants takes a turn putting forth flowers. If you sow seeds or transplant flowers like cosmos, sunflowers, marigolds, zinnias, *Gomphrena* (globe amaranth), celosia, and others periodically throughout your season, it will extend their overall bloom time and presence on your rooftop. Are you looking to sell cut flowers? Home in on flowers that give you the local advantage. For example, cosmos and sweet peas are annuals that perform well on a rooftop but are terrible to ship—all the better for you if you're cutting them to take directly downstairs to your home, or by bicycle across the neighborhood to deliver to a local restaurant.

Native flowering plants are touted as a great rooftop crop. But despite their adaptation to your overall regional growing zone, the native plants won't thrive if those you select fail to match the rooftop site's microclimate. Before you choose, check that your growing medium drains or dries the way your flowering choice likes it and that the amount of direct light your roof receives is tolerable to your plant picks. Keep in mind that planting native plants often means you're providing a food source for native (and introduced) insects. Be prepared for what a busy lunch counter looks like! Shredded leaves, stems covered in insects, and fruit picked clean from the plant—to me, this sounds like a success story. But it will change the appearance of your rooftop garden landscape.

Select flowers for beauty but also for bloom time, height, maintenance required, and disease and pest tolerance. These native wildflowers are easy, long-blooming, self-seeders with big height for their shallow media depth needs.

GROW WITH THE PROS

Stephen Orr

AUTHOR OF *THE NEW AMERICAN HERBAL*

WhatWereTheSkies
Like.blogspot.com

Few gardeners have better green thumbs than experienced author Stephen Orr. Here, he shares his best tips on a favorite plant group: herbs.

For fifteen years I grew hundreds of plants in containers on my eighth-floor rooftop garden in West Chelsea in NYC. One of the easiest (and therefore my favorite) all-around groups of plants to grow, way up there in the intense sun and drying winds, was herbs. Here are a few I can't live without.

- Bee balm (*Monarda didyma*) is another good tea plant. It's full of thymol, a natural antiseptic. Called Oswego tea, from the days when early settlers saw Native Americans using it, the plant has earned another name, bergamot, because the scent of its leaves resembles bergamot orange, one of the primary ingredients of Earl Grey tea. Perennial.

- Fennel (*Foeniculum vulgare*) is another celery relative. I almost always go for the dark-leaved fennel variety since its purple-brown foliage looks great as a backdrop to a group of pots. Butterflies love the yellow flowers in midsummer, and you can always grab a few leaves or flowers to add to any recipe or salad where you want a hint of anise. Like lemongrass, this useful plant is supposed to soothe the stomach (as well as freshen the breath). Annual.

- Lemongrass (*Cymbopogon citratus*) makes up for its grassy, lanky appearance with its leaves' strong lemon scent. It's valued in Mexico and India (and many other places) as a tea that soothes upset stomachs. But it's also good in cooking, especially in Southeast Asian cuisine, or sprinkled in regular black tea. Tender perennial.

- Lovage (*Levisticum officinale*) is very close in appearance and flavor to celery. The smoky, almost curry-like scent of its leaves makes it indispensable in my kitchen. You need to add only a few snips to lentil soup or roasted root vegetables to appreciate the flavor. A tall plant with yellow Queen Anne's lace-type flowers, it requires a large pot where it has room to grow. It was once thought that to drink or bathe in lovage would attract love. Perennial.

- Thyme (*Thymus* spp.). There are many varieties of thyme, and all of them do well in the sunny, exposed conditions of a rooftop. Some of my favored types include lemon thyme, woolly or mother-of-thyme (which makes a good groundcover), English thyme for cooking, and any of the beautiful pink, mauve, or white-flowered types that look great spilling out of a strawberry pot in midsummer. Try not to plant them in persistently moist conditions, since the plants can be prone to mildew. Perennial.

Composite flowers like the sunflower provide hundreds of blooms for nectar and pollen seeking insects, then grow pounds of protein–rich seeds for birds. Cheerful and easy to grow, these are a great starter plant for the bird–and–bee friendly rooftop garden.

The rooftop gardening world is divided on birds: there are those who love them and those who see them as pests. I'd like to put in a few kind words for birds, since they play an important role in seed dispersal, insect management, and urban beautification. For years I have watched with great pleasure as migratory birds make use of our fall flower seed heads as a calorie-rich fuel for their flight south. We also have local year-round residents, like the mockingbird who rattles off every song it knows as I climb the stairs to the Eagle Street Rooftop Farm to feed the chickens breakfast.

If you provide a food source, you'll see birds flit in and out throughout certain times of days and seasons. If you assess your rooftop more comprehensively, adding to your rooftop design with the four bird basics in mind—food, water, cover, and shelter—you'll see more birds, more often. If you're also a bird nerd like me, here's what you need to do to create a landscape they'll like:

Food. Birds specialize in their use of seeds and nuts, fruits, insects, nectar, and pollen for food. If you are planting nectar flowers, check the bloom times for full-season coverage. Research which flower works best for the birds in your area. If you are planting berry, nut, or fruit shrubs and trees and are willing to share, look into summer, fall, and (vital for year-round resident birds) winter-bearing plants. If you don't want to share, please use bird netting with a fine enough mesh that the birds don't get entangled when they dive in for food.

Water. It's moving water birds enjoy best (and the movement will keep mosquitoes from laying eggs—not the winged animal you hoped to attract!).

Cover. Most birds feel safest when provided a quick and accessible place to hide from potential predators. Grasses, shrubs, and evergreens are strong landscape plants for creating cover.

Shelter. Shelter includes access to nesting materials (either plant-based, or human-donated materials like yarn and hair), winter protection in four-season locations, and a good spot for mating and baby bird rearing. Perennial shrubs, trees, and rooftop garden features like trellises are perfect for perching. Evergreens and trees with lingering deciduous leaves make for good winter shelter.

Attracting Wildlife to Your Rooftop

Inviting populations of insects (like butterflies) and animals (like birds) up to your rooftop is a narrative, not a sound bite. Before putting out a token hummingbird feeder and a butterfly bush, take the broad and more logical approach:

Go native. Plants at home in their ecosystem will be good partners for insects in your region and for the birds that feed on those insects. Look for local seed savers and native plant nurseries as sources of seeds and plants.

Start small. Plant a few varieties or species to see which flowering plants thrive and seem to be attracting the most insects. In your planting plan, include several different flower species known to provide both nectar and pollen to the insect you're hoping to host.

Plan the full season. Look up the bloom times of your plants and aim to have something in flower at each point in the growing season.

Grow the species, not the cultivar. Native or not, many of the most lovely flowering plants have been selected, bred, hybridized, and genetically modified to be just that—beautiful. Among the many other traits lost in the beauty-first shuffle is the ability (and need) to provide significant nectar or pollen for pollinator populations. Some common ornamental varieties of plants, such as double-petal sunflowers and even *Buddleja*—the butterfly bush—can be similar "neutered." Look for open-pollinated, seed-grown native cultivars. It's a mouthful, but basically it means plants that maintain the flower shape (and if relevant, berry size) and leaf color of the native species.

Skip the sprays. Pesticides kill insects, and rarely just the ones you mean to harm. This is true even for organic-certified sprays such as pyrethrins, spinosad, and rotenone, which kill beneficial insects and so-called pests alike. Horticultural oils and insecticidal soaps, used accurately and with specific targets and timing, are less detrimental.

Get to know your insects. The relationships between plants and insects are complex and dynamic. Insects have their own foraging patterns, dietary preferences, and flight behavior, such as how far from home base they'll fly. Some insects are floral generalists; others have deeply ingrained preferences for flower color, structure, bloom time, and height. These specialized needs don't change quickly, any more than humans could develop the ability within a generation to survive only on oak leaves if all the lettuce in the world was eradicated. If we lose these pollinators, we lose the plants: for plants that rely on insect pollination, their flowers develop nonviable seeds or none at all. If you are rooftop gardening in an area with insect species that are oligolectic (preferring just a few plant species) or monolectic (dependent on one plant), look up their plant partners and grow them if you're able!

Growing Rooftop Trees

Trees are splendid plants and should be recognized as lifelong friends. Depending on the species you select, trees can serve as a food source for you as their gardener, or for animals, birds and insects throughout the year. Trees can provide shade and windbreak. Trees provide year-round visual interest with their growth habit, bark texture and color, and leafing out cycle. Although its growing environment and cultural care will influence the shape and appearance of any tree, many have a genetic predisposition toward one shape or another, described as oval, columnar, pyramidal, vaseshaped, round, clump, weeping, or conical. The tree you choose should be one whose changes you look forward to year after year, whether watching its delicate leaves flush out come springtime, or enjoying the harvest of fruits and nuts in the summer and fall. Finding the right tree for your site is a compromise—or agreement!—between what you're looking for and your tree's natural preferences. Your rooftop microclimate will influence how well the tree handles the stress of confinement to a container or green roof system.

HOW TO PLANT CONTAINER TREES

Container–bound trees can survive a while, but for the long term, planting trees on a rooftop requires thinking ahead. Here, open bottom containers are used atop the preexisting green roof system at the Battery Park Rooftop Garden— a perfect system for the trees' reaching lateral roots.

Done well, trees thrive on rooftops. Following the steps outlined below will ensure a less-stressed, healthier plant. Some municipalities require that trees be affixed to the slab, particularly in green roof applications. Check before you plant!

Select a container two to three times as wide as the root mass of the tree, and at least as deep as the container the tree is currently in. Make sure your new container has drainage holes. To protect the roof, use a saucer below the pot. If you choose to use drainage aggregates, line the container with a separation fabric between the aggregate and the growing medium.

To avoid damaging the tree during transplanting, use gravity: every time you're tempted to lift, tug, or pull, think whether you can instead slide the tree into place. Check that the trunk and leader (the main branch you've selected as the central stem of the tree) are upright and centered. Halfway through filling the container with growing medium around the root ball, water it thoroughly. Allow the water to sink in, then finish adding or removing growing medium. Check that the crown of the tree (the area where the trunk meets the roots, often encircled by a scar on grafted trees) is at least an inch or two above the soil, and not buried. This can lead to disease problems.

Especially during its first growing season, water your tree well. Mulch the surface of the container to keep moisture in and protect the roots, as well as keep pests away.

During the tree's first winter, particularly in low-volume containers, protect the tree's roots by wrapping the container. Burlap or a heavier-duty material can be used. Pruning and fertilization depends on the type of tree; as a general rule, prune in the late winter or early spring, and stop fertilizing well before the onset of frost, to allow the tree to go dormant.

An orchard thrives thirty–five stories above street level at the Battery Rooftop Garden thanks to open bottom containers allowing the trees to access the green roof system below.

Selecting Trees

Trees are not impulse projects. Over its lifetime, a tree will need more water and more room for its spreading root system. Keep in mind, a tree's canopy mass is matched, if not exceeded, by its root system. Most tree root systems grow far wider laterally than they grow deep. This quality makes trees suited for the shallow medium profiles of rooftop gardening but also serves as a word of warning about their tenacity! Every precaution should be taken to ensure that the tree's developing, water-seeking roots don't damage the rooftop membrane. Avoid trees known for water-seeking roots (sorry, sweet gum!).

Ask your local nursery about dwarf or container-friendly tree varieties, and explain your weight load limitations. The weight of your tree includes its root ball, bole, and crown,

HOW TO KEEP ROOFTOP HONEYBEES

SMOKER

HIVE TOOL

HIVE

If you aren't sure you have the pollinators you need to support your rooftop fruit crops, beekeeping is a practical, engaging, and rewarding addition to any rooftop garden or farm. Not all crops need honeybees for pollination purposes, but bees generally will ensure higher fruit set. As a bonus—or primary purpose—honeybees make honey. The small footprint of an apiary compared to pounds of honey in yield is unmatched by almost any other potential rooftop-produced crop.

There are two essential considerations to ponder before beekeeping. First, it may not be legal in your municipality: check the regulations. Additionally, check your rooftop's weight load capacity. The weight of a hive is a function of the style of hive and the amount of honey the bees have foraged. Each frame of honey can weigh between four to six pounds, and each beehive super—the individual boxes of a Langstroth hive—can contain eight to ten frames. In a successful season in a standard Langstroth-style hive, the weight of the honey harvest alone can be between 90 and 120 pounds. A full beehive of honey, honeybees, and larva can weigh up to 300 pounds.

Assuming these are not barriers, beekeeping for beginners starts off most smoothly with a community of helping hands. Seek out a local professional or practiced hobbyist beekeeper. Ideally, you have a mentor who can answer questions and calls, assist with your first few swarms or harvests, and compare notes on difficulties and diseases. Consider the costs of beekeeping, which can run from one-time purchases of gear to annual costs associated with feeding, replacing, and caring for your bees. Finally, take a deep breath and do some honest soul-searching about your temperament. Your ability to work through heat, smoke, stings, and surprises with focused, calm, steady motions will pay off in less risk on a rooftop and, with the right honeybee population, fewer stings. When done well, beekeeping should feel rhythmic and centered.

The ideal rooftop site has eastern exposure for most of the day, to make the most of the morning light and warmth. A wind block of some kind is helpful, particularly if your rooftop experiences strong winter winds. A flat, open surface is ideal for the hive and for your agility to work as the beekeeper. Make sure the access you have to the rooftop allows you to carry the beehive supers safely.

At L.A.'s Pizza Romana's rooftop garden atop a parking garage, pomegranates thrive in containers hugging the parapet wall. Read more about this garden in Chapter 8.

the weight of the container, and the saturated weight of the growing medium. When calculating the weight of your tree, remember that weights on a roof are calculated as per square foot at each contact point. For example, a tree with a three cubic-foot ball and bole (a footprint of three feet by three feet, or nine square feet) that weighs three hundred pounds conveys a load of 33 pounds per square foot (300 pounds divided by nine). Given time and the horizontal room to grow, the weight load of a tree may actually decrease per square foot as its root system and canopy spread.

If you aren't propagating the tree yourself, you can purchase trees as a transplant. They are typically available as bare-root, container plants, or balled and burlapped. Each transplant style has its advantages. Bare-root trees may present a wider selection, as you may be able to find more trees available by mail order or online than at your brick-and-mortar local nursery. While smaller at first, bare-root plants will often catch up to and surpass their container-grown colleagues within a few seasons. On the other hand, it can be useful to survey in person the actual specimens of container or balled and burlapped trees at a local nursery. For trees that require dramatic pruning cuts at the beginning of their first few years, the novice grower benefits from a good nursery's choices in selecting leaders and training branches. Look for any dry, damaged roots and branches, including poorly done, jagged pruning cuts. Check for collaring, coiled, ensnarled roots, or roots emerging from the container at the bottom. Examine the tree for insect or disease damage.

When purchasing trees—and definitely if you're attempting to propagate from a cutting—be aware that many trees come from grafted stock. Grafted trees are the marriage of the roots of one type of tree to the trunk (and branches, flowers, and fruits) of another. This is most commonly practiced with fruit trees, where the desirable qualities of the produce benefit from a more robust rootstock. If a grafted tree is not identified at the point of sale, look at the base of the trunk for an encircling scar as evidence of a graft. Rootstock selected for dwarf qualities do best in tight quarters. Look for fruit

UP ON THE ROOF

Battery Rooftop Garden
NEW YORK, NEW YORK

Founded in 2010

Thirty-fourth story green roof with container garden

Total rooftop space: 2,000 square feet

Total planted space: 1,860 square feet

BatteryRooftop Garden.org

New York City is famously a melting pot of migrants. Each spring, they come from the shores of the Panama Canal dressed in black and gold, or find their way from the mountaintops outside of Mexico City. In the fall, they return from the north in dizzying numbers and spend a few weeks gorging in the world's greatest foodie town before frost pushes them south. These are our birds and insects, of course: among others, Baltimore orioles and monarch butterflies. In flight above Lady Liberty's high-held torch, these migrants have been tracing the eastern seaboard for longer than human history.

Thirty-four stories above Wall Street and Manhattan's southernmost harbor, a rooftop oasis offers shelter and respite. Within its secluded 0.05-acre footprint, the Battery Rooftop Garden hosts 160 species of plants, including evergreens such as white pine, beautyberry (*Callicarpa*) shrubs, and flowering plants such as crocuses that use the sheltered microclimate of a steel-framed pergola to bloom early each spring. There are vegetables for the gardener, of course. Fruit trees, berry bushes, and herbs are seamlessly integrated into the landscape. But the most striking feature of the rooftop can be seen by looking up close. Woodpeckers visit the apple trees. Warblers flit quickly in, then out, then in again on the hunt for some of the many insects that make their home in the perennial plantings. Pillbugs lumber through the rich, moist soil, living fossils in a thoroughly modern place.

To see the garden's installation, turn to pages 38–39.

trees grafted onto M27, M9, and M26 rootstock, all of which are suitable for dwarf and container growing.

Unless there is a specific reason you need a larger tree immediately, trees benefit from transplanting at a younger age and smaller size. They'll cost less and be easier to transport and lighter to carry up the stairs. When transporting your tree from nursery to rooftop, aim to keep the roots from drying out, and avoiding nicking or snapping the branches and bole. Damage on a small tree can cause serious problems that will be magnified over time.

Long-Term Tree Care

Because a tree is a long-term perennial, the growing medium should also be carefully chosen to suit the tree's preferences. Before choosing your growing medium, research the right blends specific to the tree's pH range, drainage, and fertility preferences.

Mulching around your trees will help retain moisture, vital for establishing healthy trees on a rooftop. Mulch is applied a few inches away from the trunk of the tree, not near the crown. Three inches is standard for on-ground mulching; an inch is sufficient on container plants.

The chart shown on the following page describes the general soil type and pH preferences of some common fruit trees, as well as a few tree-specific best practices for care. You'll want to keep these preferences in mind as you select your growing media and containers. For example, while our rooftop peach tree can stay outdoors, wrapped, during the New York City winters, a tree such as a lemon would likely have to be carried indoors each cold season.

Tree Preferences, Soil Type, and pH

TREE	IDEAL PH	IDEAL GROWING MEDIA	TIPS
Apple	5.0–6.5	Well-drained growing medium is best. A slightly acidic potting soil is fine.	Dwarf apple varieties do well on rooftops. To ensure pollination, plant more than one of two different varieties that bloom at the same time. Alternatively, seek out grafted varieties of two or more apples that share a trunk.
Apricot	6.0–7.0	Rich, light growing medium; tolerates moist soil if well-drained. A compost-enriched potting soil is best.	Apricots, peaches, and nectarines do poorly with early spring pruning in cold weather. Prune in the summer, removing wood that has just fruited. As new shoots appear, prune them off to keep all side branches at least four inches apart.
Avocado	6.0–8.0	Rich, well-drained growing medium; low salt tolerance. Fruiting avocados do better in deeper containers.	Sprout a tree from any commercial pit by suspending the seed using toothpicks over a cup of water, so that the bottom of the seed stays wet and can swell, crack, and germinate. Be aware that the resulting tree will carry characteristics of the parent trees, whom you've never met.
Cherries, sweet and sour	6.0–7.0 and 6.0–7.5	Light, well-drained growing medium.	Most modern hybrids are self-pollinating, but double-check with your plant nursery. Sour cherries tolerate heavier soils and partial shade; sweet cherries do best in full sun on a warm site.
Figs	6.0–6.5	Can tolerate most growing medium types as long as they are not acidic.	Figs are easy growers. If you're feeling ambitious, prune the roots to force fruiting. Shoots that pop up near the base of the trunk should be clipped off. These, set in soil with the aid of a rooting hormone, will take as new trees.
Lemon	6.0–7.0	Well-drained, evenly moist growing medium.	Lemons are warm-season plants and will need to be overwintered indoors if growing in a four-season climate.
Peach and nectarine	6.0–7.5	Well-drained light growing medium that will warm quickly in the spring; light fertility.	As with apricots, prune new growth after fruit has set during the warm season.
Pear	6.0–7.5	Loamy to heavy growing medium; can tolerate poor drainage to some degree.	Don't be alarmed if during the early part of the season, fruit fall all at once. This natural thinning allows for better fruit growth on those that hang on. Be careful not to let the tree dry out when flowers and fruit are setting, or they'll drop.

1N	HERBS	1S
2N		2S
3N		3S
4N		4S
5N		5S
6N	KALE (LAC'I)	6S
7N	RADISHES	7S
8N	ENCORE—	8S
9N	—LETTUCES	9S
10N	2010 MUSTARD MIX	10S
11N	RADISHES	11S LETTUCE
12N	MUSTARDS '11	12S ARUGULA
13N	MUSTARDS '10	13S MUSTARDS
14N	SPINACH	14S CARROTS/RA
15N		15S

*It is common sense
to take a method and try it.
If it fails, admit it frankly
and try another. But above
all, try something.*

FRANKLIN DELANO
ROOSEVELT

7

Planning Your Planting

Given the limited space of a rooftop garden, it's useful to think through your planting plan before you get started. A planting plan includes both a map of where your plants are going to grow and a loose outline of their growth over the season. I call this a "space-time" map because it includes both the physical space where the plants will go as well as the time they'll spend there over the growing season.

In an annual planting plan, this includes when crops are seeded and transplanted, when they start to yield, and when they're pulled to make room for cover crops or another plant in a crop rotation. Even perennials have a place in a space-time map. As they grow over time, you'll want to show their gradual encroachment, and decide to prune or cut them back to keep space available for other plants. If you're in the process of designing new beds, laying out a green roof, or setting up an irrigation system, a space-time map can help define what you'll need as bed dimensions and irrigation points.

Making a Planting Plan

Don't think that the word "map" implies you have to be able to draw. Nor do you have to include all this information straightaway on your map! These details are easily conveyed in a table form, and many online tools are now doing the mapping for you. The important thing is to start to think ahead. You'll find that a planting plan, even if it always stays mental, is the easiest way to organize and maximize your rooftop growing space.

Traditional Space-Time Techniques

You can maximize your growing space by using long-standing gardening and farming techniques up on the roof. The key to success is an understanding of the principles behind each practice. Then, you can easily start to swap out crops for those with similar characteristics. Here are some principles you can use to guide your plan. Feel free to improvise!

Succession planting. Plant once, then plant again! There are many reasons to practice succession planting. Fast-growing vegetables like salad greens, radishes, peas, beets, and bush-type beans are easy crops to sow every two or three weeks. Slower-to-yield crops like carrots and long-term leafy crops like kale and Swiss chard can also be seeded or transplanted several times throughout the year. Short-burst harvest crops

To learn more about succession planting greens like microgreens and baby greens, turn to page 174.

SUCCESSION SOWING: SPACE-TIME PLANTING PLANS

You can map out your rooftop garden any number of ways, but one of my favorites is a space-time map. The top map shows lettuce greens and chili peppers sharing a green roof raised bed row in April, May, and June. The middle map is the same plan limited to a single container. The bottom map illustrates a different crop plan: a container started in lettuces, the center lettuce harvested and replaced with a long-season fruiting crop (such as a tomato or eggplant), and finally the same fruiting crop (shown as a blank circle) grown to encompass the container, surrounded by new transplants (such as new lettuces or basil, shown as small green circles).

like cherry tomatoes can be transplanted twice in a season a few weeks apart so that at the end of the year when the first planting is slowing down, the second planting matures later and carries fruit through the end of the season. Succession planting is at the heart of successful hydroponic greenhouse growing, where a limited plant palette makes the most of a year-round growing environment by providing a constant, consistent yield.

Crop failure is another reason to use succession planting techniques. If you have to pull a plant, have seeds handy to fill in the space. When we have crop failure with our cucumbers because of a freak heat wave on the rooftop, we're ready to jump in and direct sow with a good heat-tolerant stand-in, like a slow-to-bolt greens mix or a quick planting of late-season dill. A nice list of ready-to-go seeds to have on hand to plant includes microgreens, radishes, and short-season carrots; annual herbs like dill and cilantro; and fast-germinating mint family herbs like mint, basil, and anise hyssop. Count the days left before your frost-free days, and if the number is greater than the days to harvest of your back-up crops, plant away!

Generally I sow and then resow troublesome crops once a week to every ten days until the insecure period (fluctuating weather, hungry animals) is over. This is particularly true in my growing zone for seeds like spring crops, when soil and air temperature fluctuate during the seeding period for crops like peas, radishes, and lettuces.

The following table is a sample of the chart I use at the Eagle Street Rooftop Farm to determine how often to sow, then resow, our annual vegetable crops.

To make this table your own, write in your own frost-free and frost dates. In New York City, zone 7b, we generally plant cold-tolerant crops at the frost-free date on 4/15, and the more sensitive crops such as tomatoes or cucumbers after any serious danger of irregular cold weather has passed, one month later. You can find "days to maturity" listed on the seed packet of each crop, or online. The duration between intervals is up to you, although generally one to three weeks is standard for root, leaf, and short-season fruit crops. For

Repeat Sowing Example, Eagle Street Rooftop Farm

FROST-FREE DATE = 4/15   **100% FROST-FREE DATE = 5/15**   **FROST DATE = 10/20**

SAMPLE PLANTS	SEED OR TRANSPLANT?	DAYS TO MATURITY	INTERVAL BETWEEN SUCCESSIONS, IN DAYS	1ST PLANTING	2ND PLANTING	3RD PLANTING
Beans	Seed	55	10	06/01	07/11	N/A
Cucumbers	Seed	50	21	05/20	06/03	06/24
Kale, chard	Transplant	60	21	05/01	05/22	06/12
Radish	Seed	26	7	4/15	4/22	4/29

long-season fruit crops, such as melons, peppers, tomatoes and squash, generally two to four plantings each season staged ten to fourteen days apart will give them time to mature within the growing season.

Plant varieties that mature at different times. Another space-time technique is to stagger your harvest throughout the season by transplanting different varieties of the same plant with varying days to harvest. For example, transplant-ing an early jalapeño (sixty days to green, seventy days to red ripe) at the same time as a Tabasco pepper (eighty days to red ripe) yields peppers in waves, not an overwhelming explosion!

Intercropping. There are multiple benefits to intercropping, from pest management to nutrient compatibility. Here, you are looking to match crops that mature at different times. For example, while waiting for your tomatoes to grow fruit, you can plant lettuces around them. By the time the lettuce heads are ready to pick, they can be harvested and pulled out, roots and all, to make room for the maturing tomato plant. Or plant a crop that does well in the shade, like radishes or microgreens, between rows of tall trellised cucumbers. The key to intercropping for yield is to avoid plants with allopathic relationships: alliums and beans, for example. Try to put those two together and you'll see stunted growth instead of increased yield! Intercropping is different from companion planting—although they share many characteristics—because intercropping focuses on yield, whereas companion planting focuses on the relationship between plants, particularly as related to pest management. (Companion planting is explained more fully in Chapter 8 in the context of pest management.)

Intensive planting. Small-scale market gardeners have been cramming plants too close together for centuries. With the often-limited space of rooftop growing, close-cropped planting methods can grant higher yields while testing the limits of too-close quarters. Use a square-foot planting frame to follow these spacing recommendations:

1 PER SQUARE FOOT	2 BY 2 PER SQUARE FOOT	4 BY 4 PER SQUARE FOOT	6 BY 6 PER SQUARE FOOT
Broccoli, cabbage, cauliflower, cucumber, eggplant, pepper, tomato	Corn, herbs, kale, lettuce, potatoes, strawberries, Swiss chard	Beans, beets, peas, spinach	Radishes, carrots, cover crops, microgreens

Another handy method of determining spacing is to use your hand as a measuring tool. Some transplants can be planted a hand's length apart, others at your fingertips when the fingers are spread out into the "surf's up," "rock on," and "peace sign" positions. Generally, these represent eight-inch, six-inch, four-inch, and two- to three-inch distances. When I don't have any other tools with me, I find this to be the most expedient way to space my planting.

Thinning removes over-sown or too closely planted crops.
Thinning over-sown crops in a timely fashion will prevent plants from slowing their aboveground growth. Thinning can be done by carefully pulling out the young plants, cutting them down with scissors or a harvest knife, or transplanting out the extra seedlings. With the exception of crops toxic in their young stage (tomatoes, for example), many young thinned seedlings are edible. For example, slender carrots and radishes are eaten whole (taproot and leaves); tender herbs like fennel, parsley, and basil become a flavorful garnish; and edible greens from many plant families like kale and lettuce are tasty when tiny as well.

Use your handiest tools to remember approximately six, four, and two inch planting distances.

Turning Failure into Success

Some crops are more challenging to grow on a rooftop than others. The stressful growing conditions of a rooftop can thwart the growth of successful taproots, promote (unwanted) early flowering, or change the flavor of a sweet crop to a bitter one. But there are a few strategies to turn lemons into lemonade.

Many plants have edible plant parts that, while they weren't your initial intention to grow, are perfectly delicious as a substitute. Taproot crops like carrots, beets, and radishes that fail to develop a taproot can be enjoyed instead for their edible stem and leaves. Radish flowers and seed pods are edible. Carrots, left to overwinter, flower in their second year as an edible, sweet, delicate, lace-like bloom.

GROW WITH THE PROS

Bill Shores

**FOUNDER,
SHORES GARDEN
CONSULTING**

ShoresGarden
Consulting.com

Maximizing Chicago's growing season is paramount for rooftop gardener Bill Shores. For his tips on planning your planting, read on.

Since I began gardening my interest has always been ways to maximize crop yields in small spaces. My initial training was in French Intensive Gardening, a technique that emphasizes meticulous bed preparation and plantings spaced closely together to form a canopy over the soil. This is an excellent way to increase crop yields while decreasing weed pressure and soil moisture loss. I tend to favor grow boxes. They are lightweight, come in a variety of dimensions, and are typically four to ten inches deep. Lettuces and many other salad greens will happily grow in four to five inches of a mix of peat moss, compost, and perlite.

Let's say the chefs I work with have requested I supply them with one hundred three-inch-tall heads of baby pak choy weekly for a special dish. I select three grow boxes that will accommodate one hundred small heads of pak choy each. I know it will take five weeks from seed to three-inch pak choy heads. Here's how it works:

- In a separate grow box, all of the pak choy seedlings are grown for three weeks.

- The three-week-old seedlings are transplanted into three grow boxes, spaced farther apart so that they can grow larger than in the crowded seedling grow box.

- I start another round of seedlings in the original seedling grow box.

- Two weeks later, the three hundred mature pak choy heads are ready to harvest. One week following the harvest, I can transplant the second round of seedlings into the three grow boxes I harvested from.

What works with this system is the precision. I like being able to grow crops in exact quantities and sizes so I can easily switch crops as needs change; I also like the space efficiency and the visual impact of well-grown container crops.

Some crops take more nutrients and greater soil depth than a rooftop can provide. But quite a few of these can be eaten as shoots. Few plants emerge from the soil as beautiful as corn, which presses up as a single leaf curled in a tube that holds pearls of rainwater and morning dew like a scoop of ice cream in a cone. At no taller than four inches, corn shoots are incredibly sweet and can be eaten root, shoot, leaf, and crunchy, germinated seed. Likewise, hops as mature plants are a tenacious grower, the roots of which can do serious damage to a rooftop if not grown with care. But when trimmed back annually to the quick, the young shoots that reemerge each spring are edible, with a delicate, asparagus-like taste.

Fruiting crops like watermelons, cucumbers, and squash require a good deal of water to grow, and the help of a pollinator traveling between their male and female flowers to bear fruit. Smaller in volume but delightful in flavor, the edible flowers are a nice stand-in when you have no fruit.

Raw in a salad, candied on a cake, or suspended frozen in an ice cube, edible flowers are easy to grow. For their abundance and tolerance of the rooftop microclimate, try arugula, anise hyssop, bean blossoms, bee balm, broccoli (if you missed harvesting as a tight head, then fully blooming, butter yellow, and beautiful), borage, calendula, chrysanthemum, dianthus, lavender, marigold, mint, nasturtium, pansy, pea blossoms, sunflower, and violets.

Wind, dry growing conditions, and heat can cause climbing crops to struggle on a roof. Grown closely together, as one would with microgreens at an inch or two apart, a crop like peas can instead be harvested for the shoots. The tendrils, leaves, stems, and flowers are all edible. As a bonus, after inoculating the pea seeds with the right nitrogen-fixing bacteria (for peas, *Rhizobium leguminosarum*), you can intercrop pea shoots between tomatoes and other heavy feeders to help feed their reaching roots.

If your heat-sensitive herbs produce flowers and seeds, eat them instead of the leaves. Dill, oregano, sage, basil, thyme, and many others have delightful edible flowers and poppy-size, flavor-rich seeds. Cilantro bolts to produce fresh green coriander seeds.

Rooftop Crop Rotation

Don't be overwhelmed by the number of maps, plans, and schemes for crop rotation. The theory is simple. Moving annual plants around in a pattern keeps you one step ahead of disease, and avoids overdrawing your soil nutrient bank. Gardeners and farmers group their rotations by plants that share disease susceptibilities (often delineated by plant family) or make the same nutrient demands of the soil (these groups are referred to as "heavy feeders" or "light feeders").

A rooftop garden is no exception to these principles. In a limited growing space, where pest and disease pressure can take over quickly, it's important to be strategic. And it's certainly worth thinking about nutrient depletion, as limited soil fertility is one of the biggest challenges of rooftop gardening. Whether you are working in containers, container beds, or green roof rows, as long as you're growing with annual plants (especially edibles), crop rotation will bulwark your garden against easily prevented problems.

Setting Up a Crop Rotation Plan

Crop rotation plans are abundant, but you may not see one that matches your exact plant list. Luckily, they all follow the same basic tenets:

Keep host plants out of reach of disease and pests for longer than the disease or pest can survive without a host. Disease and pest problems often haunt plants in the same genus or family. The best crop rotation plans will keep plants with the same disease susceptibilities out of a given planting space for five to six years, or about the time it takes for most fungal pathogens to die off for lack of their host food. Insects that overwinter or pupate in soil will return the following year, so even simply changing crops annually helps.

Don't overdraw your soil nutrients . . . Another common practice is to follow a heavy feeder with a light feeder. For example, corn, tomatoes, and cabbage are considered heavy feeders; herbs, root vegetables, and most greens are considered light feeders.

SETTING UP A CROP ROTATION PLAN

A typical crop rotation divides beds into four or more groups, depending on how your crops group together based on the principles described below. You can apply these same ideas to container gardens by visualizing clusters of the containers as shown here.

. . . and redeposit nutrients when you can. Planting a "giver" crop regularly in each bed or container is a proactive way to amend soil. If space allows, this can be a green manure or cover crop. If your rooftop has no space to be fallow, edible crops like plants in the Fabaceae (legume or bean) family should be worked into the scheme. Plants in the Fabaceae family host beneficial bacteria on their roots, and in exchange for plant sugars, the rhizobia affix and make atmospheric nitrogen accessible.

Be open to observe and adapt. Most crop rotation plans focus on clean, crisp rotations of three to four groups of plants. In a true poly-crop garden, however, life is rarely so simple! If mapping your entire plant list seems overwhelming, focus on where nutrient deficiencies and disease pressures are likely to arise or currently seem most prevalent, and let defensively preventing or fighting back on the offense lead the direction your crop rotation takes.

If you must monocrop, do so wisely. You would not be the first person whose love of tomatoes keeps them planted in your biggest and best container for far beyond the recommended number of seasons. If that's the case, aim to at least switch varieties every few years, and pay close attention to other disease prevention options like maintaining good air circulation with pruning, soil health with compost topdressing, and best pest control through cultural and biological methods.

Fitting in perennials. Astute readers might notice in observing the world around them that many plants, from trees to grasses, survive just fine without rotation. Many perennials produce chemicals that act as natural pesticides, and they have woody tissue to protect them from insect pests. Perennials have also evolved to find partners in disease prevention. Some of these multiseason plants produce root exudates that attract beneficial fungi that form a protective sheath around the rhizosphere, crowding the lunch counter to the exclusion of detrimental bacteria, fungi, and nematodes. Others grow specialized plant organs like nectaries. Without all the reproductive trappings, this type of extrafloral growth produces nectar attractive to territorial insects like ants, which will fight off other insects to defend the tasty food source. If a perennial plant is wisely chosen on your rooftop site, it will stand as the exception to the rotation rule for many seasons to come.

Planting Into the Fall Season

Moving into the fall season, there is still time for a second set of planting on your rooftop. But you have to plan ahead! Count backward from your first frost date to the planting date of these crops. If your rooftop has a shady microclimate, these plants may be slower to mature. Leafy crops and roots are your best bet, as they will produce an edible plant part in time. Fruit, flower, and seed crops may not mature before shortened daylight hours and frost.

Crop Rotation: Plant Families

FAMILY	INCLUDES
Bean (Fabaceae)	Beans (soy, bush, garbanzo, broad, fava, wax, lima, pole), cowpeas, mimosa, sweet peas
Beet (Amaranthaceae)	Amaranth, beets, spinach, chard
Cabbage (Brassicaceae)	Broccoli, brussels sprouts, cabbage, cauliflower, Chinese cabbage, collards, cress, kale, kohlrabi, mustard, nasturtium, radish, rutabaga, stock, turnips
Carrot (Apiaceae)	Anise, carrots, caraway, celery, coriander (cilantro), dill, fennel, parsley
Cucumber (Cucurbitaceae)	Cantaloupe, cucumber, melon, pumpkin, squash (summer and winter), watermelon
Mint (Lamiaceae)	Basil, mint, rosemary, sage (and other square-stemmed herbs)
Onion (Amaryllidaceae)	Chives, garlic, leeks, onions, scallions, shallot
Tomato (Solanaceae)	Eggplant, peppers, potatoes, tobacco, tomatoes

Planting Into the Fall Season

PLANTS THAT MATURE IN 30 DAYS	PLANTS THAT MATURE IN 60 DAYS	PLANTS THAT MATURE IN 90 DAYS
Arugula	Basil	Brussels sprouts
Beets (small)	Bush beans	Cabbage
Radishes	Broccoli	Collards
Microgreens: mustards, spinaches, lettuces	Carrots	Cauliflower
	Cilantro	Parsnips
	Collards	Peas
	Green onions	Rutabaga
	Kale	
	Kohlrabi	
	Leeks	
	Lettuce	
	Swiss chard	
	Turnips	

UP ON THE ROOF

Roberta's Restaurant Garden

BROOKLYN, NEW YORK

Founded in 2007

First-story rooftop container garden

Total rooftop space: 655 square feet

Total planted space: 320 square feet

RobertasPizza.com

The garden at Roberta's has an eclectic design. The "rooftop" portion of the garden is on top of two shipping containers that host raised beds two and a half feet wide by twelve to eighteen feet long by two and a half feet deep (the false-bottom beds hold two-feet-deep soil above a six-inch drainage layer of broken Styrofoam). These are designed to have hoop-house covers. A third shipping container supports a permanent greenhouse made of framed wood and greenhouse plastic, which is used to start seedlings. The rest of the garden is container-based, using food-grade plastic containers from a local brewery, two and a half by three and a half feet, and two to three feet deep. They can be easily moved by a pallet jack.

Everything the garden grows goes to the restaurants below: Roberta's and its highly praised tasting room, Blanca.

Melissa Metrick, head gardener at Roberta's in Brooklyn, New York, takes great care to select crops that will make a unique impact on the restaurant's menu. Here, papalo, a pungent herb reminiscent of cilantro, is cut, weighed, washed, cleaned, and prepped for service. To keep ground–level customers up–to–date with what's growing, a chalkboard sign announces the latest roof harvest.

Harvesting

On a rooftop, the best time to harvest is early in the morning before the heat of the day wilts your crops. If your only time to harvest is at night, water the plants first, then either prepare and eat the harvest straightaway or keep it cool until you're ready to use it. Don't be shy about harvesting, either. Many edible crops benefit from constant harvesting. For example, pruning off the tips of basil encourages side shoots to grow. Picking cucumbers and summer squash quickly and early encourages the plant to continue to flower and fruit.

How to Harvest Taproots, Tubers, Rhizomes, and Bulbs

These underground crops are the bearers of stockpiles of stored sugars (carbohydrates and starches) made during a good growing season's worth of photosynthesis.

Taproot crops (carrots, radishes, turnips). Taproot crops pop their "shoulders" out of the soil when mature. Their harvest-size circumference should look similar to the familiar circumference of the carrots and radishes you've seen at the farmers' market. For taproots that remain buried, trace your finger around the top of the root. If it feels bigger than a nickel or better, a quarter, it is likely ready to be harvested. Fortunately, these taproots can be eaten at any size, greens and all. They may be small for several reasons. They may be getting too much sun and not enough water. The container or bed soil temperature may be too hot. Finally, they may need to be thinned. Each should have its own two inches of space. Make a "peace sign" gesture with your fingers to measure between the roots and see if they're far enough apart.

Tubers and rhizomes (potatoes, sweet potatoes, yams; ginger). Tubers' leaves die back when the plant is ready to be harvested. The stem turns brown, wet, and flaccid. Gently and carefully use a hand trowel or a spading fork to ease the tubers out of the soil. If you planted them in a mound or a

deconstructable container, pull the side open and let the soil spill out onto a tarp.

Bulbs (garlic, onions). The leaves of alliums (garlic, onions, scallions, shallots) die back when the bulbs are ready to be harvested. The leaves of allium crops can be eaten when young, green, and tender. If any alliums begin to make flowers (for garlic, these are called scapes), cut them back: if you don't, the energy stored in the bulb will be used up in flower production, shrinking the bulb as the flower grows. Clipping the flower back keeps the focus on bulb growth. If you're growing garlic for seed stock, harvest and let the heads dry thoroughly. Garlic is a cloning plant, propagated not from seed but from its cloves. Retain the biggest heads and separate the largest cloves, keeping the outer paper on to prevent rot. Examine the cloves for any damage or disease and discard affected heads. Store in a cool, dry place with good circulation for cool weather (fall season) planting. In my experience, growing successful garlic on a rooftop requires rich soil and good irrigation.

How to Harvest Leaf Crops

Leaf crops are among the easiest and most rewarding plants to grow on a rooftop. Plants just love to make leaves, so it's hard to go wrong. In periods of heat, stress, or longer daylight hours, some leafy crops will lengthen at their stems and send forth flowers. This process, called bolting, uses up sugars stored in the plant's roots, stem, and leaves. You'll taste the difference! Curtail this process by succession planting your leafy crops, and getting rid of the ones that are bolting. You can also snip off the flowers and continue to harvest the crop, up to a point—you'll know when to stop when the leaves become too bitter to eat.

Square-stemmed plants (basil, mint, thyme, oregano). Square-stemmed plants are in the mint family (Lamiaceae), and can all be harvested generally the same way. Rather than removing the largest leaves, for a small amount of leaves,

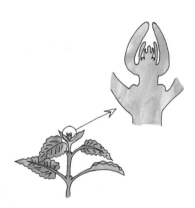

As long as the tip of the plant's main stem is intact, the growth of the plant's lateral buds will be suppressed. Removing the apical meristem (the hormone control center at the tip of the plant's new growth) will release the lateral buds to send out new branches. This creates a bushy, globe–like growth habit, rather than a long, reaching plant with fewer leaves.

pinch from the top of any stem on down. For larger bunches, go down the stem to the next set of new leaf growth and harvest above that. This type of harvesting produces a pattern of growth that is similar in appearance to a family tree turned upside-down. Once removed, the side shoots will grow and you will end up with a bushier plant. On a rooftop, this family flowers quickly. Pinch back. You'll get better flavor and higher yields.

Leafy greens such as kale and Swiss chard. Harvest the outer, lower, largest leaves. Pick the leaves right at the stem, snapping or cutting them down to leave a clean scar.

Head lettuce, cabbage, bok choi and other head crops plus kohlrabi. Pull out the entire head. Cut or prune off root to either put into compost or turn it back into the bed. If composting, shake off excess growing medium first: you want to keep all the soil you can on your rooftop!

Cut-and-come-again microgreens. Usually done twice. Cut low on the first cut to avoid stemmy bits in the second cut. For faster regrowth (but slower harvest), cut around new baby growth. Use a knife blade to flick or wipe off detritus as you cut. Wash well, especially low-growing spinach.

How to Harvest Flowering and Fruiting Crops

When seeds mature inside a fruit, hormones are activated, signaling that the propagation process has succeeded. In response, the plant will begin to scale back its flower and further fruit production. On the rooftop, harvest early and harvest often!

Winter squash and melons. There's all kinds of advice about thumping, smelling, and examining squash and melons on the vine. Here's a trick: look for the tendril growing closest to the fruit. If it is withered and brown, the plant vine has started to cut it off, and the fruit is ripe and ready!

TOP Rather than picking the largest leaves, pinch or prune the tips of herbs to encourage new growth.

BOTTOM Microgreens are closely grown, stunted versions of larger greens such as kale, lettuce, and arugula. Cut to just above the newest growth, harvesting two or three times off the same plant before pulling and resowing.

Cucumbers, zucchini, peas, and beans. Left on the vine, cucumber and zucchini will grow to unabashed proportions. Beans and peas will become swollen, then dry. These are fruit crops that should be picked as soon as they're ready— ripe, but still tender! These fruit will gain water weight, but that adds little to flavor. Unless the crop is a variety selected specifically to be harvested at a larger size, cut small and cut often. Pruning away fruit before the seeds are allowed to ripen encourages more flower set and fruit growth. Use pruners, scissors, or a harvest knife to cut cucumbers and zucchini from the vine as soon as they are near six inches long. A good rule of thumb is to cut a cucumber when it's too big to fit in a pickle jar, and the zucchini follows at just an inch or two larger.

Flowering vegetables (broccoli, cauliflower). Harvest while buds are tight. When buds start to open, the head will quickly go to flower and lose its taste and suitability for cooking. This can happen in the course of one hot afternoon! Harvest one head, then wait for smaller side-shoot heads.

Nightshade fruit crops (tomatoes, eggplants, peppers). It can be tricky to guess the harvest-readiness of hard-skinned peppers and eggplants. Size is a good indicator. Ripe tomatoes usually harvest easily with a firm pull. Peppers all start as green and ripen to specified colors. Eggplants are best harvested by the mature size indicated for each type.

YOUR TOOLKIT

Part of budgeting out your year includes the tools you need to get growing. Rooftop farming will never require a tractor, but the right set of hand tools can go a long way toward making your garden grow more easily.

All rooftops

- Closed-toed shoes
- Sunscreen
- Pruners
- Hand trowel
- Tarp
- Baskets, buckets
- Rain gauge
- Thermometer

Green roof row farming

- Scuffle hoe
- Bow rake
- Narrow flathead shovel
- Optional: compost corkscrew

Tools—especially wood or metal—should be cleaned with each use. For regular cleaning, mix a five-gallon bucket of sterile (not beach) sand with three-quarters of a quart of mineral oil (or motor oil). Tools can be dipped in after each use then wiped down with a rag. The grit will gently wipe away soil, and the oil will protect and waterproof your tools.

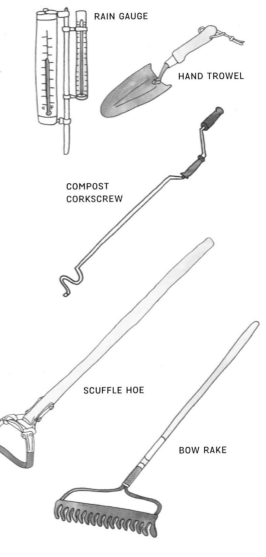

RAIN GAUGE

HAND TROWEL

COMPOST CORKSCREW

SCUFFLE HOE

BOW RAKE

CLOSED-TOED SHOES

"Cover crop" is an umbrella term for plants, typically grains and legumes, that are grown in rotation with other edible plants to give soil a chance to rebuild its nutrient bank and tilth. Cover crops do this in two ways. Most cover crops are grown for a season in a fallow field, then turned under into the soil. As they break down, their biomass feeds the decomposer community, which releases the nutrients they've gained. All that digging, eating, and secreting helps open up air and water flow in the soil, too. Some cover crops are winter-hardy; others die back during the winter, making it easier to turn them under in the spring.

Legume cover crops, such as vetch and clover, additionally host bacteria on their roots that affix atmospheric nitrogen. It is these that I recommend on the rooftop. First, it's hard to turn under cover crops in the traditional sense on a green roof or in a container garden. Unless you have incredible microbiology in your peat moss mix, the plant material will take a long time to get broken down. Second, nonleguminous cover crops take, not give, nutrients from the soil while growing. The only payback comes when you till them under. This is hard to do properly on a rooftop, even a green roof, since generally speaking the insect population microbiology isn't rich enough to break down the cover crop quickly.

As we learned, rooftop cover cropping requires good space and time management. At the Eagle Street Rooftop Farm, I plant a legume blend of hairy vetch and crimson clover seeds in the late summer or early fall, giving the plants enough time to establish before the frost. They are dormant through the winter, but return in the spring. We then go through the farm "harvesting" all of our cover crop. Some of the green tops go to the chickens, some to the rabbits, and a good deal to the compost bins. A container gardener can use the same approach. Be sure to inoculate your leguminous cover crop seeds with the appropriate rhizobia. You should be able to get an inoculant from the same source where you buy your seeds. It's unlikely the bacteria are already present in large numbers on your rooftop.

Cover crops are an important part of a green roof farm landscape. Clover persists through the snow as late as early February, providing a rich source of greens for our rabbits while their roots provide sugars under the snow to nitrogen–fixing bacteria.

*We are dealing
with a vital, living system
rather than an
inert manufacturing
process . . . the gardener's
aim is not to protect
sick plants but to
enable healthy ones.*

ELIOT COLEMAN

Rooftop Pests and Problems

On a rooftop as in every growing space, plants will
exhibit signs of stress. The long game is to steadily
increase plant health with proactive choices, not
defensive bandaging. A rising tide raises all boats: if you
focus on the rooftop system as a whole, you'll be able
to bring your plant health up to peak performance with
systematic, steady improvements. This is an approach
that requires some up-front research, commitment,
and a bit of patience. Your plants will start to see
themselves through pest and disease pressures
robustly supported by systems you've set in place.

At times, even with the best planning and practices, your rooftop garden will experience temporary, seasonal cycles of nutrient, disease, and pest pressures. There are a number of simple, proactive steps to take to mitigate how profoundly they affect your garden. Here, we will discuss only organic practices. Time and again, organic methods for my own rooftop sites have proven to be a stable, predictable, and decreasingly input-intensive way to grow. With these practices, we follow in the footsteps of generations of gardeners and farmers who have successfully used beneficial insects, crop rotation, pest traps, and organic, plant-derived sprays, oils, and powders sparingly to treat pest and disease problems. Your plants will benefit when you protect the diverse ecosystems of microbes and insects by targeting the interlocutors with care. Finally, rooftop farms and gardens are typically located above residential or commercial spaces in densely populated areas. It seems most respectful of the safety of the humans below to avoid using chemical applications of any kind.

Establishing Your Tolerance and Practices

I will admit that in early growing seasons we suffered round after round of pests, as the most tenacious of pioneering insects found their way up to us. Flea beetles pinpricked scattered bites on the eggplant and arugula leaves. Aphids, in frighteningly increasing numbers, latched onto the new growth of our kale and tomatoes. But over a few seasons of employing cultural, physical, and biological controls, we rode out most of the problems and now have a more firmly balanced ecosystem on our rooftop site. Cultural controls included checking mistakes we were making as growers, from timing our planting incorrectly to simply planting the wrong plants for our soil and site. Physical controls meant literally blocking pests, using methods from handpicking to covering crops or the growing medium with a row cover or mulch product during times of year when pests were at their peak. Biological controls meant finding ways to roll out the red carpet for beneficial insects. Biological controls also included spraying or applying organic pesticides and fungicides, minimally and with the right timing to make a difference, rather than in a panicky blanket application. Of all of these methods, the last we used the least.

Before we get started listing problems and solutions, it's important that you assess your own tolerance for pest and disease damage. In my own growing practices, I've always tolerated a little damage as long as the part of the plant I want to eat remains unchecked in production—and edible. For example, I don't mind a certain amount of hornworm (*Manduca quinquemaculata*) damage to the leaves of my tomatoes later in the season, as long as tomato fruit production is in full run. Early in the season, when the tomatoes are smaller and just setting out leaves, I have the time to handpick the hornworms off and drop them into a bucket of soapy water. At this stage, tomatoes need all the leaves they can get to gather up the sugars needed to set the fruit I want to eat. However, as the season goes on, we're busier. It's impractical to handpick tomato hornworms when so many other crops are calling for our attention. Instead, we've made sure to include in our planting plan flowers in the Apiaceae family. These lacey, multibloom flowers of herbs like fennel, cumin, dill, and anise (avoid those that take two years to flower—biannuals, such as carrots) begin to bloom in late July and into the fall, providing a lure for the adult braconid wasps (Braconidae) whose larva parasitize the tomato hornworm when they lay eggs on its fleshy green back. Conveniently, the braconid wasps begin to take over pest patrol duties during the period of the year when we're too busy to handpick hornworms. Now, on a rooftop this happened neither naturally nor quickly: we had to strategize, and even then in our case it took three seasons to get the characters in place on our rooftop three stories up in the air. This process required deep breaths on my part as the anxious grower (*it'll take time, but it'll work out!*), as well as research (understanding who eats whom, and when) and a commitment to the long term over instant results.

As another example, I used to avoid planting Swiss chard on the rooftop. The problem started in our first growing season, when a warm spring and wet two months in June and July had caused an explosion of our leaf miner population. Leaf miner is an umbrella nickname for the larvae of various flies, each particular to a group of crops. In our case, it was the maggots of the fly *Pegomya hyoscyami* happily eating a tunneling maze through the layers of our chard, spinach, and beet leaves, defecating along the way. Held up to the sun, the translucent patterns in each leaf were marred by coffee-colored blockages where piles of poop were now stashed. While caterpillar damage of any sort with its nice, clean bite marks can actually serve us well when selling to chefs as proof of organic deliciousness, the shit-filled, swirling loops left by maggots is a harder sell. One staff member observed that it looked like stained glass, but that didn't ease our conscience. After that season, spinach and beets (in the same family as chard) were determined to be too slow for their per-square-foot value. Because of the leaf miner, we also cut Swiss chard out of the planting plan entirely, turning instead to other leafy greens. But our market suffered (people miss those colorful stems!). Working it back into our planting plan meant observing the cycles of the leaf miner with a closer eye. If we were vigilant about pruning off the damaged leaves early on, we removed the maggot with the leaf while it was still munching away. This stopped them from being able to drop into the soil to pupate. Although we had a few weeks of damage through mid-May, by late June we'd removed all the infested leaves, all the maggots, and thereby the source of adult fly pests. The up-front work in the spring was a hassle, but paid off in protecting later crops. A second set of young chard later in the season made it through without a single nibble: the leaf miner cycle had been broken by our steady eradication, and when temperatures rose over the summer, the fly stopped returning to lay her eggs. The following spring, no overwintered population rose from the soil, and we were ahead of the game with less work to do, thanks to the effortful work of the previous season.

When your rooftop garden starts to suffer from pest problems, disease pressure, and nutrient deficiencies, it can feel frustrating. Many gardeners throw in the trowel when a plant isn't meeting their expectations or an insect population overwhelms their rooftop. Don't feel antagonized by your plants! Treat these problems as an opportunity to gather clues about your plants' larger needs, adjust and amend, and strengthen your garden as a healthy growing space. Plants don't speak, per se, but they certainly communicate clearly when something in their ecosystem is awry. As ever, knowledge is power: learning to recognize the circumstances, timing, and cause of a problem will help you become proactive, not defensive, on your roof.

Cultural Problems

If your plants keep dying, it is likely that a number of factors are contributing to their demise, nothing easily dismissed with a silver bullet. It takes a lot to kill a plant, and if it's really that bad, it's usually traceable to a combination of basic cultural failures. To address all of these, you need to use silver *buckshot*.

Cultural problems are frequently at the root of pest, disease, or nutrient deficiency issues. Cultural practices are the choices we make as growers in creating the living environment for our plants. If a plant can't stay healthy, it could be that we haven't given it the right growing environment in which to thrive. With our cultural practices corrected, plants stand a better chance of facing down disease and pest pressures at full strength.

Best Cultural Practices

Cultural problems are caused by the way gardeners interact with their plants. Checking that you've put the right plant in the right place, that you've provided the correct growing medium, irrigation, and fertility for its nutrient needs, and assessing the growing system as a whole (everything from microclimate factors like sunlight and wind to your choices of container or bed depth) will help troubleshoot where the overall problem is derived from.

Start with the soil. Healthy soil is the foundation of plant health. Choose and cultivate a growing medium that has good pore space for air and water. Avoid a growing medium that compacts at first or over time, as this inhibits both the movement of water and air, but also the success of the plant's roots and their attending microorganisms! To prevent nutrient deficiencies, check that the medium is the right pH so that nutrients are accessible to the plants. When growing annual crops like vegetables, be aware of what's being taken from the soil with each harvest and what you need to do to replace it.

Choose the right plant for the right place. Before planting, learn more about the light and soil requirements of the plants you'd like to grow. Test a few! Over seasons of experimentation, keep track of the plant species and cultivars within the species that were successful to your standards, and aim to grow them again. Sample new varieties of crops until you have a broad plant palette that thrives on your site.

Buy healthy plants. Purchasing a transplant is a quick and easy way to get your rooftop garden growing. But don't forget you're buying a full package: the cultivar choice, pest and disease issues of the transplant, as well as the cultural practices and problems of the grower who grew them first! Before you buy, look for plants from a nursery display that seem well cared for. Examine the roots, which should not be visible growing outside the pot—if they are, that's a sure sign the plant has been container-bound for too long. Consider the plant's coloring, looking specifically for signs of a nutrient deficiency (pale leaves; underside, upper side, or leaf tip discoloration, or even discoloration along the veins) or disease (uneven brown, yellow, or white coloring). Check the underside of the leaves for insects. If the plant has flowers, pinch them back to encourage rooting and leafing out once transplanted. Perennials, trees, and shrubs root out best when purchased dormant, so look for closed buds. Ask if the plants were raised using organic practices, and if not, what was applied. Over time, try to develop a relationship with a plant grower whose seed choices and propagation practices you trust.

Plant with smart timing. Pest and disease pressures cycle throughout the season, often predictably. As insects go through their life cycle, they follow different eating patterns. You can often avoid pest problems simply by moving your plantings forward or backward a few weeks. (Recall the discussion of my own practices under "Establishing Your Tolerance and Practices.") This planning process isn't total guesswork. Many insects that interact with edible crops are deeply influenced by seasonal changes in temperature. If temperatures are lower than normal, these insects develop later. If temperatures are higher, pest pressure rises earlier in the season. Long ago, farmers realized that by tracking and predicting seasonal temperatures, they could project the emergence of various insect pests, craftily altering their planting plan to anticipate when pests might be at their most voracious. The method evolved into a useful formula called "planting by degree days." Your local agricultural cooperative extension office is likely keeping this tally (as of this writing, the University of Illinois at Champagne-Urbana's Prairie Research Institute has an easy-to-use calculator on their website). My favorite way to anticipate pest problems is by following the time-honored practice of phenology: the observation and record-keeping of key moments in the life cycles of plants, insects, and animals. Noting the correlations between these events lends predictability to your season.

Likewise, to avoid fungal diseases or the stress brought on by midseason heat, try adjusting your calendar to plant around wet or dry periods of the year. Planting the crop, then planting a new round of the same crop later in the season, will help determine the best timing for each crop.

Keep it clean. The plant world is a dirty place, and that dirt is rich with microorganisms necessary for plant health. What should be kept clean are your tools, containers, and anything else that may harbor the pathogens you're trying to avoid. If you just finished ridding your rooftop of cucumber vines covered in powdery mildew, run your gardening gloves through the wash and dip your pruners in a 1:10 bleach solution.

LEFT Heat damage on a tomato plant. Pick the fruit, pull the plant, and start again.

RIGHT Particularly common during periods of heat or long daylight hours, "bolting" can be curtailed by pruning down flower stalks as they appear. Eat (or sell!) these flowers!

Common Cultural Problems

Sun and heat damage. At the outset, the microclimate of your rooftop is likely to lean toward too hot to handle. In leaf crops, too much heat causes bolting. Root crops will be underdeveloped. In fruit crops, heat damage can cause fruit to dry out, blister, or crack. Consider light-colored sub-irrigated containers, shade cloth, and planting heat-tolerant crops. Everything helps: for the roof, resurfacing the rooftop to any color other than black; for the plants, providing good irrigation and a rich (while not too heavy!) growing medium.

Bolting. Plants want to produce seeds to survive. In periods of acute stress, they will use their stored sugars from photosynthesis to produce flowers and then seeds. As mentioned earlier, the sugars are used up in flower production, leafing out slows and the leaves become less sweet and often more bitter or spicy. While this is smart and good for the plant itself, it's a problem for the gardener who wants to eat them! To prevent bolting, use seeds selected for slow-to-bolt qualities, plant bolt-prone varieties in the cooler shoulder seasons, and harvest

plants by cutting to the quick rather than picking only the outside leaves. If bolting has already begun, cut the flowers off at the base of their stem. We've found the most practical way to avoid bolting is to constantly harvest our leafy greens to the quick, removing the leading tip of the plant at the end of the main stem. In salad greens, herbs, and foliar crops, the removal of the leading tip of the plant removes the hormone that suppresses lateral growth. This causes side growth to shoot out, keeping the plant in continual leafy production over flowering.

For Rick Bayless' Frontera Grill in Chicago, tomatoes in earthboxes are protected from the lake effect off Lake Michigan by custom designed wind screens.

Wind damage. Wind damage causes desiccation—the drying out of both your plants and the growing medium. Well-chosen perennial crops can bear up and acclimate to wind; damage to annuals can be tempered with windscreens. Cold winds will cause browning of the leaf margins. In this case, as long as the young leaves appear green and healthy, wait it out: the new growth will likely come in just fine as the seasonal temperatures warm up. The more seriously windy roofs should use a mulch, both to retain moisture as well as to keep the dry growing medium from blowing away. In circumstances

UP ON THE ROOF

Pizza Romana

LOS ANGELES, CALIFORNIA,

Founded in 2009

Two-story rooftop container garden

Total rooftop space: 10,350 square feet

Total planted space: 700 square feet

DivinePasta.com

CubeMarketplace.com

Full-CircleGardening.com

Pomegranates, eggplants, and lemon trees on a rooftop? Sounds like an Eden. But maybe the better word is oasis: one thing to know about the Pizza Romana Rooftop Garden in the warehouse district of downtown Los Angeles is that it's *hot*. The air simmers above the treeless sidewalk. Walking up the gentle slope of the approach ramp to the top level of the parking garage that hosts the rooftop garden, the asphalt radiates heat that you can feel through the soles of your shoes. Lora Hall, the site's gardener, works dressed in serious sun protection: long pants, a long-sleeved shirt, and a wide-brimmed sun hat.

Because the structure below was designed and engineered to have parking on the roof, the roof's weight-bearing capacity and drainage—it is at a slight pitch—is excellent. Planters were built all around the perimeter of the roof using reinforced cinderblock with wood faces, at three feet deep and ranging in length from about ten feet to almost forty feet. Additionally, the owners removed a few rooftop parking spots to install a garden of six one-foot-deep raised beds, each six by three feet. Hall uses these for annual crops, focusing on favorites from Italian cuisine to satisfy the chefs she works with, taking into account the aforementioned heat—which is so intense that during one growing season, the tomato plants' fruit actually cooked in their own skin.

Likely the hottest garden in this book, Pizza Romana uses reflective gravel and deep, water–retaining beds to keep the crops cool(er).

where natural or installed irrigation is sufficient to allow the competition for water, rooftop growers can use a living mulch, like a cover crop, around their plants. The more soil covered, the better plants will handle wind damage.

Frost damage. In a four-season climate, frost is inevitable. At the end of the season, most growers anticipate frost by watching the weather. Fruit crops get harvested before the frost; many fall leaf and root crops (kale and carrots are just two examples) are hardy enough to ride through a few light frosts. More damaging is the frost that is followed by warmer temperatures, which causes the iced water frozen inside the plant cells to expand, rupturing the cell walls and exposing the plant to bacterial infections, softening, and bruising. Freak frost in the spring is worse. Leaves may look bleached, blistered, cracked, or scorched along the margins. As with wind damage, ride it out and hope for younger, healthier growth. Frost damage on fruit trees can make blossoms turn brown and fall off. This is irreversible damage and leads to less fruit. Protect plants from early frost damage with row cover, cloches, or cold frames. Be careful to tent the material above the plants, not letting it touch their leaves, stem, flowers, or fruit.

Incorrect planting. One of the most common cultural problems is choosing the wrong plant, or planting the right plant the wrong way. Timing, spacing, depth—the junctures where you could go wrong abound. Don't be frustrated. The forgiveness of annual agriculture is in constantly trying again, even several times within a season.

Incorrect watering practices. When it's raining, and until the soil has time to dry out a bit from the rain, turn off your irrigation system. If after a rainstorm the saucers under your plants are full of water, empty them. Watering practices do and should vary from site to site. On a hot roof with a lighter, particulate-based growing medium, you'll have to water the same plant more frequently than a cooler roof with a growing medium rich in organic matter. On a hot roof that grows dry-soil-loving lavender, you'll water less than on a hot roof where you're trying to coax a juicy melon to thrive.

A common problem with container gardening is compaction. Watering tends to cause the container soil to settle, and drainage worsens. So does airflow, and plant health suffers as the roots are starved for oxygen. For this reason, many lightweight mixes contain particulates such as perlite, vermiculite, gel soil polymers, and sand. Each has its own pros and cons. Perlite rises to the top of the mix over time. Vermiculite is very fine and works best in combination with other materials. Gel soil polymers hold moisture but also tend to hold onto it, rather than sharing it with the potting mix. Sand adds weight. Experimenting with various growing media will help you determine which works best for your site.

Salt buildup. Brown, dry leaf tips and edges, the buildup of a white crust on your container or the top of your growing medium—these are signs of salt buildup. This generally comes from one of two sources. One is synthetic fertilizers, which use salts as a delivery method for the essential nutrients. The other source could be your water. Softened water contains sodium chloride, the worst salt for plants. It is generally recommended to avoid irrigating with soft water entirely. Removing salts from container soil is as simple as watering the container heavily, then allowing it to drain fully before saturating it again two or three times. Check after a week or so to see if salt crystals continue to appear on the container. Flushing containers this way also removes nitrogen, so if the salt buildup continues, consider treating the cause and not the symptoms. Test your water, examine your fertilizing regime and the products you use, and consider altering course!

Nutrient Deficiencies

Particularly with annual, edible crops, it's your job to keep the nutrient balance healthy for your crops. Drainage and erosion can cause nutrient loss over time, but so does regular plant growth. Plants remove elements from the soil and assimilate them into their tissues. For example, most of the weight of a tomato plant is derived from hydrogen and oxygen from water, and carbon from the air. But its nutritional value draws heavily from essential nutrients the plant draws up from healthy soil. These include the familiar nitrogen, phosphorus, and potassium, and also trace elements such as iron, zinc, boron, manganese, and copper.

Sometimes it's not a lack of nutrients, but a lack of access, that causes deficiencies. Nutrients can "lock up," becoming unavailable to plants when the moisture, air, temperature, and pH of your potting mix or growing medium are not ideal. The presence and health of soil microbes and the balance of available soil nutrients also affect how well plants can take up nutrient ions. Of course, this varies plant to plant, but in general the following hold true:

Moisture. Too little water makes it hard for nutrients to dissolve; too much leaches the nutrients out of the soil entirely.

Air. Poor airflow—as found in compacted, waterlogged, or heavy (overly clayey) soils—changes soil chemistry. The lack of oxygen damages the balance of microbes in growing media, turning the growing environment to aerobic from anaerobic.

Temperature. Temperature changes microbe behavior. At the cooler ends of a season, microbe activity slows down, which in turn diminishes the amount of available phosphorus and nitrogen in the soil. It may still be present, but until the microbes render it accessible to plants, your soil tests will read low in N and P. Hold off on applications, especially as oversupplying nitrogen can cause damage downstream in the watershed. There's not much you can do to change soil temperature, but if you plan on testing your soil to determine any amendments you should use, do so during the season when soil temperatures are well into a constant average above 68°F, a happy temperature for most microbial activity. You'll get readings truer to your growing medium's needs.

Soil pH. Soil that has gone above or below the ideal pH range for the plant exhibiting nutrient stress is the most common cause of soil nutrients becoming "locked up." Either acidity or alkalinity can bind up nutrients.

Nutrient interactions. Finally, the available quantities of nutrients play off one another. It is likely that the soil you first use in your containers or for your green roof will have been manufactured to be a balanced mix. However, your amendment practices over time will likely—slightly and slowly—modify the nutrient content of the soil. This is one of the many reasons to read and follow closely the fertilizing instructions on any product you use.

Identifying Nutrient Deficiencies

ELEMENT	WHAT IT SUPPORTS IN A PLANT	WHAT HAPPENS WHEN IT'S MISSING
Nitrogen (N)	Leaf and shoot growth	Pale foliage, stunted growth. Older leaves, then younger leaves, may develop reddish or yellow discoloration.
Phosphorus (P)	Root growth and seed formation	Red or purplish coloring. Stems short and slender. Yellowing of leaves. Stunted growth.
Potassium (K)	Flowering and fruiting, tissue strengthening, woodiness	Scorched leaf tips. Reduced fruiting and flowering.
Magnesium (Mg)	Chlorophyll formation	Older leaves show yellowing between veins and around edges.
Calcium (Ca)	Formation of plant cell walls	Primarily affects fruit: blossom end rot or core rot common. Foliage may be reduced in size or distorted.
Iron (Fe)	Chlorophyll formation	Leaf yellowing on young leaves, mainly between veins.
Manganese (Mn)	Chlorophyll formation	Leaf yellowing between veins on young leaves, sometimes with small dead spots.

UP ON THE ROOF

Print Restaurant Rooftop Garden

NEW YORK, NEW YORK

Founded in 2011

Sixteenth-story rooftop container garden

Total rooftop space: 6,400 square feet

Total planted space: 600 square feet

RecoverGreenRoofs.com

Print Restaurant in Manhattan's Tribeca neighborhood turned a rooftop swimming pool into a rooftop garden. The gardener, Meghan Boledovich, uses a wild food forager mentality to tackle the persistent weeds that integrate into her vegetable and herb crops. With their hardy botanical qualities and strong, assertive flavors, rooftop weeds provide a welcome punch of flavor for the chefs. Cultivars of arugula, dandelion, mâche, sorrel, and minutina are all close to their weedy ancestors and are easy to grow rooftop crops.

What makes a plant a weed is subjective, as many are ornamental, others edible, and many the most adept survivors on your rooftop. If weeds are making you mad, keep in mind the old adage: one year's seeding means seven years' seeding. Catch your weeds early, and don't let those tenacious seeds develop!

Companion planting is a cultural practice that will profoundly help your rooftop garden. It is a long-established technique of using the natural relationships of plants to other plants, insects, and microbes in a way that benefits both your garden's mini ecosystem and your yield. On a rooftop, it's useful to think about companion planting in the following ways:

Plants that share nutrients. In a container, bedding, or row, match a fruiting crop with a root or leaf crop. By pulling on different nutrients, they won't overdraft on what's available in a well-balanced growing medium. By the time the fruiting crop has started to flower and fruit, the leaf or root crop (lettuces or carrots, for example) can be harvested and the fruit crop topdressed to give it a boost toward harvest.

Plants that deposit nutrients. Legumes, in particular, make great companion plants. Their capacity to affix atmospheric nitrogen through their partnership with rhizobia bacteria make them a great partner plant for almost any heavy feeder. The traditional Native American planting of corn, squash, and beans follows this by matching the heavy-feeding corn with beans, a member of the legume family. Be sure to look up which bacteria matches with the legume you're using before inoculating your seeds.

Plants that share light and shade well. Tall plants or trellised plants that cast shade can be planted with an understory of shade-loving crops; for example, in the spring, peas intercropped with radishes; in the summer, tomatoes with lettuce below.

Plants that attract good insects. Over time, more and more pollinators will find their way up to your roof. But in your first season of planting crops that need pollinators, such as cucumbers, you'll need to roll out the red carpet and put up a billboard bigger than just their small yellow flowers. Plants that are particularly attractive to pollinators and also usefully edible include those in the Apiaceae and Lamiaceae families. Plant them in container clusters or rows near the plants you'd like pollinated. Additionally, good insects include those that attack the bad insects. Companion planting includes growing alluring flowering and non-flowering plants known to host insects who parasitize or eat pests. For example, the braconid wasp loves the open-faced blooms of the fennel flower. Rather than eat the fennel bulb, allow some to bloom, and eat the leaves. Plant densely near tomatoes to attract the wasps that eat the tomato hornworm.

Plants that deter detrimental insects. Plants have an enormous amount of tannins, toxins, and other chemical weapons in their arsenal to defeat insects. Tender edible crops are less well-rigged than the mighty oak, however. In general, bitter or strongly flavored plants such as marigolds and mints can help deter pests from eating more appetizing crops. Any root-level pests can also be mitigated if they're sharing the same container and growing medium. Before planting, look up the exact relationship and its function: for example, although alliums are an excellent pest repellant, they can be repellant to certain other vegetables as well!

Plants that act as trap crops. The most effective way to use trap crops is to plant them far away from your other plants. For example, plant nasturtium in its own bed, row, or container a good ten feet away from your tomatoes (not in the same container!). Check the underside of the nasturtium leaves for clustering aphids. Ideally, this will serve as a fine spread for ladybug larvae to dine upon, or a concentrated area for you to apply an insecticidal soap.

TO DETER	PLANT
Aphids	Coriander, chives (deters); nasturtium (attracts; plant as a trap crop distant from affected crops)
Bean beetle	Marigolds, nasturtium, rosemary
Cabbage moths	Mint, oregano, sage
Carrot flies	Rosemary, sage
Flea beetles	Catmint, mint
Squash bugs and beetles	Nasturtium, tansy

Rooftop Insects: Pests and Friends

Insect pests can slow plant growth, render plants unsightly, and spread disease. On the whole, however, if caught early and handled well, most insect damage is not a huge problem for plants: given the right growing conditions, they'll take a hit and come back swinging, often aided by other, beneficial insects. Many rooftop growers find that the overwhelming number of pests in their first and second season can be traced to the developing ecosystem. Pests are resourceful; they will be among the first to find their way to a new green space. But in short order, the remainder of the insect entourage arrives: ladybug larvae seeking aphids. Hover flies on a similar hunt. Praying mantises, omnivorous and cannibalistic. I would be more alarmed by a rooftop with no insects at all than one that seems to be bearing the burden of a pest infestation. The presence of insects is a sign that communication has begun between a once-barren space and the thriving environment of the landscape that surrounds it. Annoying, yes, but also the beginning of a several-million-year-long dialogue of which we are lucky to have a few recent speaking parts.

Preventing Insect Problems

Before you tear out your hair or your plants, run through this checklist to balance out the guest list invited to your rooftop growing space.

Get to know your plants. Spending time in your rooftop garden is hands-down the best way to manage pest and disease problems. Your observations over time will let you know if you chose the right plant for the right place or if you should switch from one variety to a less pest-susceptible one. You'll also start to note which weather conditions, seasonal timing, and site location stresses are linked to the appearance and explosion of pest pressure.

Get to know your pests. Oh boy, are there a lot of insects out there! Thankfully, your local ecosystem is likely to have a narrower, predictable cast of characters: just because it's your first time meeting them does not mean they haven't been on the block for a while. Start by using a good region-specific book or the Internet to look up the plant and its common pest problems, then set the search over again using the key insects that come up. Recognize anyone? Getting to know who is who will help with kicking them off the roof. For starters, many insect pests are host-specific to plants. (This coevolution has assured them their bread and butter for likely a very long time.) If evolution has provided a pest for your plant, it is highly likely that a beneficial insect evolved as its natural nemesis. Nature hardly ever wastes an opportunity to eat! Another reason to identify your pest and its characteristics is that pest pressures come in waves as the temperature changes throughout the year. Even the most basic understanding of their life cycle will greatly strengthen your strategy of defense or rebuttal.

Nowhere is it more important to know your pests than when using sprays, powders, and sticky traps, organic or not. A failure to understand how insects and these treatments interact leads to frustrating, misapplied cycles of overapplication, which sends ripple effects through the entire ecosystem. For example, foliar sprays that coat the leaf in an organic insecticide might work for leaf-eating insects like caterpillars. But they won't do much damage to an insect like an aphid that uses specialized tubular mouthparts to tap deep into a leaf's layers and draw out nutrients. Also, aphids are found in the largest numbers underneath leaves along the midrib. If you just spray the top of the leaf, and not the bottom, you've done little to deter their damage. Combine a few well-researched websites, a good book, and your own dedicated observation, and you're a more accurate marksman when tackling your garden's pests.

Listen closely to your plants. The chemical communication between plants and insects is the loudest silence on your rooftop garden. Plants under duress release chemical compounds from tannins to ethylene. For example, the smell of a freshly mowed lawn, which we find so intoxicatingly pleasant, is an alarm bell in the plant world: it's the grass screaming "Warning! Danger!" by releasing signaling compounds called green leaf volatiles (GVLs)—a blend of esters, aldehydes, ketones, and alcohols. When plants release these compounds, they act as the botanical equivalent of a smoke signal, letting other parts of the same plants, or plants downwind across a garden bed, know that insects have started to bite, broach, or trigger destruction of cells. Many plants are also masters of synthetic biochemistry, manufacturing chemicals to make their foliage less palatable to insects. You won't "hear" these chemicals, per se, but your sense of sight, smell, and taste will identify the auxiliary characteristics of these plant-insect interactions.

Identifying Pest Problems

DAMAGE	LIKELY CULPRIT
Holes in leaves, chewed leaf edges	Chewing insects like beetles and the larvae of flies, butterflies, or moths. Although rare on a rooftop, this also indicates slugs and snails.
Plants cut off at the base of the stem	Cutworms.
Scarred, stippled leaves; sooty mold and sticky honeydew	Sucking insects like aphids, whiteflies, thrips, and squash bugs.
Tunneling on root crops	Root–eating insects: cabbage maggot, carrot rust fly larvae. Not as common on a rooftop, but the adults can fly up, or arrive in imported growing media or with plant starts.
Wilted plants, even when watered (squash, cucumbers, melon)	Squash vine borer.
Tunnels within leaf tissue	Leaf miners.
Various fungal and bacterial diseases	Many are spread by insects. Refer to page 223 for more.

Accurately identify the problem. Treating a symptom without identifying the pest that's causing it will keep you locked in a frustrating loop. Parsing out the root of the problem breaks the cycle. For example, limp leaves often signal dehydration. But if the soil feels moist, it could instead signify that the water isn't moving through the plant as it should. Quite a few bacterial diseases, many of which are transmitted by insects, cause this kind of damage. Remove the insect, and the pathogen vector is disabled.

Identifying Rooftop Pests

Many rooftop gardeners are unpleasantly surprised to find how tremendously resourceful pest insects are at finding their way up to a rooftop. Allow amazement to take the front seat over annoyance. There are strategies to disinviting each.

APHIDS

Small, pear-shaped, its posterior spiked with two cornicles (best seen under a hand lens) that produce a defensive secretion, the aphid is likely to be one of the first insect pests to arrive in a new rooftop garden. Aphids crowd along the underside and midribs of plant leaves in vast numbers. Some fly; most don't. Depending on the variety of aphid, they come in an array of colors: red, black, yellow, and dark and pale green. Autoecious insects, each type of aphid has a plant family or cluster of crops it prefers throughout its life cycle. For example, waxy gray cabbage aphids (*Brevicoryne brassicae*) are most often found on plants in the cabbage family, whereas yellow to dark green aphids, the melon or cotton aphid (*Aphis gossypii*), prefer crops like melon and cotton.

APHIS GOSSYPII

Like honeybees, aphids can bear young without mating. Unlike honeybees, whose unfertilized eggs bear male drone bees, the virgin aphid gives birth to female young who quickly continue the population boom. Female aphids in utero can also be pregnant with granddaughters, which explains how fallout of aphids can appear to overwhelm a crop so rapidly. In their eating habits, aphids are sap-suckers, using incredibly small tubes called stylets, protected within their proboscis, to feed on the sugar-rich liquids extracted from the tissue of plants. What they're after is nitrogen, as it is heavily concentrated in a plant's newest growth. Efficient aphids target young plants and on older plants the tender tissue of buds, new growth, and growing tips. Because aphids are most attracted to new growth that is high in nitrogen, plants you are overfertilizing are especially big targets. Cut back on your liquid fertilizer applications during times of shorter daylight hours and other periods of slow growth!

To get the high amount of nitrogen their diet calls for, aphids overfeed, leaving behind a sugar-rich residue commonly called "honeydew." These sticky leftovers are in turn scooped up by many other insects, such as the lovely Brown Hairstreak butterfly (*Thecla betulae*), all sorts of ants, the recognizable common wasp (*Vespula vulgaris*, often mistaken for a bee), and a yeasty *Ascomycota* fungi group called sooty molds, whose suggestive name accurately describes the ashy appearance they cause on plant leaves. For further evidence of aphids, look for their shed skins as fine white specks on the leaves, or for the aphids themselves clustered along the underside of leaves near the midrib. Plant distress symptoms due to aphid damage manifest as leaf curl, stunted and distorted growth, and plant mortality when left unchecked.

While most gardeners are taught to use ladybugs to control aphids, just as the many types of aphids like specific types of plants, beneficial predators have a specific aphid they prefer to eat. Green lacewings will eat anything available, including all aphids. Wasp parasites like *Aphidius colemani* will do the trick on certain aphids while the wasps are in their larval stage. One important note (true for all use of beneficial insects) is that if you're growing without soil—in a hydroponic greenhouse, for example—the pupation for many of these beneficial insects involves some nestling down in the dirt. An *Aphidoletes aphidimyza* or "aphid midge" will feed on aphids as a larva for less than a week; they then need to drop off the leaf into soil to pupate to full adult. The released adults you mail-ordered will lay, but if you want to maintain a full SWAT team, make sure there are some healthy spots

Aphids, a common rooftop pest. If you haven't met one yet, you will.

for the necessary metamorphosis to adult form to happen. Other aphid control options include a soapy water wash, a hard hit of a hose at full blast to knock them off and wash off the honeydew, or the removal of the more severely infested plants (trash them—do not compost!).

CATERPILLARS

All caterpillars become moths and butterflies, which are important pollinators, bird food, and beauties to behold. However, in their youth they often inflict maddening damage on our gardens and farms. To identify the culprit, be warned that caterpillars are often known by two common names: that of the caterpillar and the subsequent name of the adult moth or butterfly. Some distinct species of insect also share common names, as you'll see. If you can, seek out the Latin name, which remains consistent between both stages. Here are some of the most nefarious on a rooftop:

Banded woolly bear, **Pyrrharctia isabella.** Handpick with care; they are prickly! Banded woolly bear overwinters in soil. Use Reemay or a similar row cover fabric to cover your containers and transplant through it in the spring to block their emergence.

Imported cabbageworm, **Pieris rapae** *and* **P. brassicae.** Handpick, generally from the underside or along the midrib of leaves, or use a row cover material to blanket crops and stop the adult from laying eggs on the leaves of the affected plants. As a spray, *Bacillus thuringiensis* (BT) is most commonly used.

Tomato hornworm, **Manduca quinquemaculata,** *and* *tobacco hornworm,* **Manduca sexta.** Handpick, or plant to attract the parasitic braconid wasp, whose larvae will eat the tomato hornworm alive when the adult lays her eggs on its ample green back as it unsuspectingly munches away on your tomato leaves.

Squash vine borer, **Melittia cucurbitae** *and* **M. calabaza.** If your squash or melon vine looks limp all of a sudden, look for the telltale "sawdust" at the base of your squash vines.

Caterpillar damage doesn't change edibility. Simply remove the caterpillar and continue to harvest.

PIERIS BRASSICAE

Squash vine borers can be removed from the stem (you can open the stem a bit more with a clean knife cut, then use the tip to flick the borer out). At a node, rebury the squash vine to encourage it to root up further and recover.

Cucumber beetle, various—**Diabrotica** *and* **Acalymma.** *Diabrotica* and *Acalymma* species' saliva often carries disease such as bacterial wilt (*Erwinia tracheiphila*) and the cucumber mosaic virus. Bacterial wilt is recognizable as a dehydrated (dry, brown, collapsing) appearance on affected cucurbits. The virus starts with one section of leaves and quickly moves throughout the vascular system of the plant. Cut the vine and gently squeeze the stem: the roping, sappy water that comes out is full of millions of *Erwinia tracheiphila*. Wash your hands and tools. Cucumber beetles are best eradicated by handpicking, keeping soil clear of leaf debris, and checking the underside of the leaves on affected plants. Sprays with pyrethrin are also effective, but must be used carefully, as pyrethrin also affects beneficials. As with other sprays, apply as regularly as the product label recommends. Note that some are applied as foliar sprays, for treatment of the beetles, while others are recommended for soil application, to affect the larvae.

Flea beetle, various—**Chrysomelidae,** *tribe* **Alticini.** A wide-ranging group, flea beetles are extremely minute, glossy insects with notably large hind legs that power their characteristic springing jumps. They are not fleas, but true beetles. On the rooftop, flea beetles easily settle in to do their worst damage on dry, sunny days. Different beetles attack different plants, but the shotgun-like bite marks left behind after they've eaten remain true regardless of genera or species. Flea beetles pupate in potting soil or green roof media with equal ease. To prevent damage to your crops, cover the soil around the plants with row cover or a mulch, so that the emerging larvae can't get out or crawl back in as they go through their half-dozen life cycles each season. Flea beetles are also parasitized by the braconid wasp, so intercropping commonly attacked plants with flowers attractive to the wasp will draw their attention

TOP Cucumber beetles' damage isn't that severe, but the pathogens they spread can be.

BOTTOM The mark of flea beetle buckshot.

CHRYSOMELIDAE

to the robust flea beetle population also available as a snack. This requires preplanning: if you know you have flea beetles, plant dill seed as you transplant your eggplants, for example.

OTHERS

Leaf miner, various. Distinctive tunneling patterns that appear in your plants' leaves as the soil warms up is the calling card of leaf miners. A general term for a large group of pests, leaf miners are host-specific. A majority are the larva of moths, flies, and sawflies. Vegetable growers typically deal with *Pegomya hyoscyami*, a grey fly fond of spinach, beets, chard, and other greens. As they eat, they deposit frass (to put it politely). The best defense is to remove the leaves as they are damaged, cutting off the infestation cycle. Row cover and sticky traps can also be used. Pesticides are generally ineffective, as the maggot is inside the leaf. (See page 192 for our approach to leaf miners.)

Leaf miner damage: the dubiously lovely frass–filled stained glass effect.

Whitefly. A sap-sucking insect that does its worst damage primarily as a disease vector (various mosaic viruses, among others), the cabbage whitefly (*Aleyrodes proletella*), silver leaf whitefly (*Bemisia argentifolii*) are common vegetable pests. Whitefly (family Aleyrodidae; 1,550 described species), like aphids, seem to jump in population from zero to sixty with ease. They are best deterred using biological controls such as beneficial insects, or organic controls like insecticidal soap or yellow sticky traps. The young population of whitefly are immobile, so at their nymph stage is the best time to wash down your plants, or treat them with a horticultural oil.

Scale insect. Scale are specialized sap feeders. The females lay living young and shelter them under their waxy body armor. Scales are easy to spot on plants, although sometimes they like to hide under the leaves. Yellow spotting, sooty molds, and a slowing of plant growth can be signs of an infestation. The best deterrence for scale is horticultural oil or a soapy wash. Several wasp species parasitize scale, but it's species-specific, so before you order them online, determine who will be the best hero to defeat your villain.

Avian Pest Control

If you see the birds below near your rooftop, you're in luck: well-adapted to urban and suburban living, these insect-eating birds can help take care of flying pests and soil-dwelling grubs on your rooftop. If you've recently weeded around your container garden tree, for example, or turned in cover crops on your green roof, you may see these birds fly in and peck around, looking for grubs, cutworms, and other pests.

Other insect eaters include year-round residents like chickadees, nuthatches, titmice, and woodpeckers; short-distant migrants such as brown thrasher, eastern bluebird, eastern phoebe, northern mockingbird, robin, and towhee, and neotropical migrants such as flycatchers, hummingbirds, kingbirds, nighthawks, swallows, tanagers, vireos, warblers, and thrushes. If your rooftop is a ready source of insects or other favored foods, these visitors might just pop up.

Avian Pest Control

BIRD	EATS
Bluebird	Small insects, spiders, insects on spiderwebs
Chipping sparrow	Small crawling insects
House wren	Small insects, spiders, insects on spiderwebs
Phoebe	Small insects, spiders, insects on spiderwebs
Purple martin	Flying insects
Yellow warbler	Caterpillars, small crawling insects

Beneficial Insects

From a lack of patience, resources, or both, many rooftop gardeners purchase and release beneficial insects. Go for it, but be advised: they may stay, they may fly away. Here's what you need to know about their habits, life cycle, and strengths on your team:

Green lacewings. It's the young lacewing larvae—known as aphid lions—whose voracious appetites lead them to consume pests such as aphids, mites, and whitefly young. Lacewings are usually ordered by mail. When they arrive, place them immediately. Spread them broadly throughout your site, scattering the eggs onto leaves near any obvious pest infestations.

Ladybug beetle. Ladybugs undergo a complete metamorphosis. Both their young and adult stages are useful to the gardener as an aphid-vanquishing solution. Ladybugs also dine upon spider mites, mealybugs, whitefly young, and scale. The larva of a ladybug looks nothing like the adult, but rather like a tiny black crocodile with reddish-orange spots. Generally, mail order ladybugs come in gallon, quarts, and pints. A pint is 75,000 ladybugs—above and beyond what's needed for any rooftop. Since purchased beetles arrive as adults and fully capable of flight, I advocate attempting to attract them to your roof rather than spending money when most of the bugs you buy will simply fly away. Ladybugs are such a common insect, most gardeners will start to see them arrive on their own a few months into a growing project. In our case, a small crop of chamomile underwent an aphid infestation, then six weeks later was crawling with the alien-esque black ladybug larvae. The loop had closed itself!

Praying mantis. These voracious beauties are indiscriminate eaters, hunting down not only pests but also beneficial insects such as ladybeetles, bees, and other praying mantises. The young feed on soft-bodied insects rather than aphids and whitefly. The mature female mantis's palate broadens to include, famously, her own male mate. This

A mail-ordered, loogie-like praying mantis egg sac.

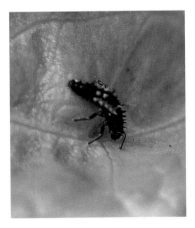

A larva only a mother could love: the young ladybug beetle.

makes mantises debatable as a beneficial, but they're beautiful, graceful predators, and if one has found its way onto your roof, feel free to handle it gently (it won't bite you) and examine its elegant structure and movements. Mail-order praying mantises will likely arrive in their ootheca, or egg-case. It looks like a loogie when fresh, and like a crusty, lightly burned marshmallow when set. Approximately two hundred nymphs live inside each one.

Spiders. Spiders are incredible predators. They're abundant and easily hosted. Because spiders are such talented climbers, parachute-style travelers, and defensive warriors, they are often among the first round of pioneers to arrive at a rooftop garden. For those still suffering from a touch of arachnophobia, remember how few of them actually bite or sting, and learn by observing them how quickly spiders shy away from your shadow, touch, or movement.

Hover fly or syrphid fly. Closely related to the housefly, these are often mistaken for wasps or bees at first glance. They are flies; they do not sting. Like flies, the young appear as white or brown maggots, and they eagerly eat up aphids as well as other small pests. Adults generally prefer pollen and hover above flowers (hence the nickname hover fly) before darting in to grab some. They cannot be purchased commercially and are best attracted by planting flowers, particularly the Apiaceae family of plants with their wide, multiflowered, umbrella-shaped clusters of blooms.

Wasps. With the exception of social wasps such as yellow jackets (*Vespula*), paper wasps (*Polistes*), and hornets (*Dolichovespula*), most wasps you'll see on your rooftop garden are not prone to stinging. In fact, wasps are important pollinators and coconspirators in pest management. Because wasps have short tongues, they will likely visit a rooftop planted with open, multiflowered plants like those in the carrot family (Apiaceae: fennel, anise, parsley, dill, Queen Anne's lace).

Further rooftop friends and heroes: aphid midges (*Aphidoletes aphidimyza*), assassin bugs (family Reduviidae), bigeyed bugs (*Geocoris* spp.), braconid wasps (family Braconidae), damsel bugs (family Nabidae), ground beetles (family Carabidae), hover flies and flower flies (family Syrphidae), ichneumon wasps (family Ichneumonidae), minute pirate bug (*Orius tristicolor*), rave beetles (family Staphylinidae), soldier beetles (family Cantharidae), spined soldier bug (*Podisus maculiventris*), tiger beetles (family Cicindelidae), tachinid flies (family Tachinidae).

Animal Pests on the Rooftop

A few years ago, burned out by the heat on the rooftop farm and looking for a few shade trees to sit under when the day's chores were done, I went to visit an old friend of mine, a farmer north of New York City up in the Hudson River Valley. As we swapped notes from the first half of the growing season, she complained bitterly about the damage done to her crops by ground-level pests. Listening to her talk was like rereading the character lists from Beatrix Potter, Brian Jacques, and J.R.R. Tolkien: deer, groundhogs, voles, moles, possums, and even the neighbor's dogs had made themselves at home in her fields.

Pausing for breath, she said at last, "I bet you don't have any problems with animals. I'd love to put my whole farm up on a roof!"

It's true: rooftop gardens tend not to have problems with the pest animals my farming friend mentioned. But every sky-high grower I know has a story to share about their first spotting of a hawk, pigeon, or gull picking through their seedlings. At our rooftop farm, three stories up in the air, each winter raccoon footprints appear in the snow around our chicken coop as they hunt for leftover grains in the fallow run. In a green roof garden thirty-four stories up, in early spring I've been startled by a woodpecker making quick looping rounds, fruitlessly seeking a tree to drill, with an eye on the tender teenage apple trees I was pruning.

LEFT Bird damage is not fatal if young leaves are untouched.

RIGHT Sticky traps are an unobtrusive, non–damaging tool (for plants or people).

Deterring Animal Pests

The approach you take with animals is about your personal tolerance and food safety concerns. The uninvited two-winged or four-legged friend that finds its way to the rooftop garden will often settle in for a while. Their persistence and intelligence can be frustrating. I've heard of a vacuum cleaner being employed to suck insect pests off plants, but for four-legged pests like a cat, no vacuum tricks will do. It's worth keeping a few ideas from this playbook in rotation:

Block them off. A wide range of materials can be used to physically block animals and insects from damaging your crops. On a rooftop, focus on using techniques that won't damage the plants (or fall off the roof!) in a high wind. Bird netting should be of a fine enough mesh to not choke or trap birds. Use barriers that allow light and water to pass through, such as a polyester fabric product. Reemay, one such product, allows for 70-percent light transmission.

With all physical barriers, be aware of when you need to remove them to allow for pollination, as appropriate.

Frighten them. Depending on your problem pest, visual barriers can get quite creative! Generally, shiny, flapping objects and false guardians like dummy snakes, owls, and scarecrows work at least for a little while. The most successful have obvious eyes or eyes that move, or they move around the rooftop.

Make awful noise. We don't hear nearly as much as animals do! Ultrasonic barriers are inaudible to humans but annoying to furry pests. On a rooftop, these are set up in the same way they are in a ground-level garden. They are often motion-triggered, so think about the place on your rooftop where a varmint might be most likely to crawl or climb up. You can't hear these devices, so you won't know when it's not working: make a practice of checking whether the battery's low.

LEFT Nylons protect apples from insect damage. Onerous application, but yummy results!

RIGHT Bird netting should be chosen for correctly sized mesh. Don't hurt your birds!

LEFT Soda pop tops used to deter birds. The gardeners said it didn't really work.

RIGHT Mousetraps provide a poison-free alternative to typical traps.

Release foul smells. You can push pests away with two kinds of smells: odors offensive to the animal, and the scent of a predator. Some plants with strong smells act as natural repellants to animals, and as long as they're not allopathic to the plants you're trying to protect, they can be intercropped in your planting plan. As for predator scents, urine is one of the more infamous pest repellants; it works best for skittish prey animals. It will work less well for the bold (like rats) and birds, whose sense of smell isn't as fine-tuned.

Ruin their meal—or invite them to dine elsewhere. If you use a foliar spray like garlic or chiles to protect your plants, you're likely going to get a taste of it, too. Be careful when you use them! Distraction planting or trap cropping is a longstanding tradition in farming and gardening. The idea is to plant a row, container, or bed that the pests can enjoy,

HOW TO ATTRACT BENEFICIAL INSECTS

Many beneficial insects will find your rooftop if the right plants are there as a food source—in addition to the pests you want them to eat, of course! Attractive plants include:

Carrot family (Umbelliferae) covers plants such as caraway, dill, fennel, lovage, and parsley. When allowed to flower, these produce beautiful, delicate umbels of hundreds of tiny blossoms and are a rich nectar source for many insects.

The square-stemmed mint family (Lamiaceae) includes all mints, catnip, hyssop, lemon balm, thyme, and oregano. Left to flower, these perennials are a treat for many beneficial insects as well as pollinators such as a wide range of bees. Be aware of their aggressive spreading behavior—plant in a confined container or section of the green roof! Tender rosemary is also in this family, although in cooler climates it must be brought indoors to overwinter. When these plants are allowed to flower, they pull sugars from their leaves and the flavor changes dramatically. The rooftop grower should decide if they are more useful as an edible crop, cut constantly, or allowed to flower as a bait for beneficial insects.

The daisy family (Compositae) includes coneflowers, daisies, and yarrow. They provide food for many insects, including butterflies. Their compound flowers welcome any visiting insect to stay a while, particularly bees eagerly packing pollen from each individual flower on the disc head of these open-faced blooms.

ostensibly so they leave your crops alone. This idea works best in larger spaces, where there's room to plant the distraction crop far enough away from your planting that they don't just line up for a second course.

Plant Diseases

In the garden and on the farm, fungi, viruses, and bacteria all can be a source of disease for your plants. Fungal infections include downy mildew, powdery mildew, fungal leaf spots, and rusts. Most fungal diseases are specific to plant parts (such as leaves) rather than systemic. Viral infections cause leaf distortion (as with cucumber mosaic virus) and yellow or white patterning and usually lead to overall poor growth and stunting. They often act in concert with one another. Bacterial infections tend to start locally in a plant, but spread easily. Symptoms often include ropey oozing, as well as a funky (some say fishy) odor at the points of infection.

The first step to eradication is identification! Knowing what you're up against will allow you to determine the timing and method of treatment, including removal of the plant if need be. The chart opposite lists characteristics to consider when narrowing down your diagnosis. On page 224, a few examples are shown. For the full scope of common plant diseases, turn to the Resources (page 239) for further reference.

Using Organic Sprays, Dusts, and Other Treatments

Organic insecticides and fungicides act in a variety of ways to control pests and diseases. Some insecticides work on contact fatally or as an irritant; some must be ingested. Some sprays and powders for fungal and bacterial problems are most effective defensively, applied on the plant before the spores or bacteria appear; others work to stop fungal

Common Plant Diseases

DISEASE	PATHOGEN	HOW IT SPREADS	WHY IT SPREADS	WHEN IT SPREADS
Powdery mildews	Fungus	Air, water	When soil is dry and/or when leaves are wet.	In spring if dry; otherwise, more often in the summer and fall.
Downy mildews	Fungus	Air, water	Humid air around leaves. Wet shoulder–season weather. Stagnant and untidy conditions.	All year.
Rusts	Fungus	Air, water, animals	Damp, warm, stagnant conditions. When leaves are left moist.	Damp periods in the fall.
Fungal cankers	Fungus	Air, water	Especially for trees, via pruning, frost, or animal damage.	All year.
Fungal wilts	Fungus	Pruning tools, infested soil, infested root material	Open wounds when spores are nearby.	All year.
Bacterial soft rots	Bacteria	Water, pruning tools, insects	When plant surface is damaged, bacteria enter.	All year.
Fungal leaf spots	Fungus	Mainly water, some air	Poor growing conditions, extreme weather.	Spring, summer.
Bacterial blights	Bacteria	Water, insects	Warm, wet weather. Excess fertilizer causing excess green leafy growth.	Spring.
Cucumber mosaic virus	Virus	Plant material, via sucking insects	Diseased seed, cuttings, or plant materials pass along the virus.	Late spring, summer.
Phytophthora, Pythium	Fungus	Soil, water	Overly wet soil conditions. Injury to plant allows access.	All year.

TOP Mold on the soil surface? Clear plants and solarize the soil if possible.

MIDDLE Thirsty? No: fusarium wilt.

BOTTOM, LEFT TO RIGHT All leaves appear discolored, but these are not the same pathogen! Beans, cucumbers, and tomatoes are from different plant families, and suffer varied disease pressures. Rust (fungus), bacterial wilt (bacteria), and verticillium wilt (fungus) are the likely suspects.

spores from germinating or to inhibit bacteria. On a rooftop, it is vital to follow the instructions exactly described by the manufacturer. Be wary of applying any sprays, dusts, or treatments on windy days or midday, when the sun is at its hottest and highest in the sky.

Organic Pest Control Products

Here are a few examples of organic pest controls available through gardening and farm supply stores and how they work. These are sold under various product names. You should always thoroughly read the instructions on the product label regarding application, use, and storage.

Pyrethrin. Derived from chrysanthemum family flowers, various powder and spray products have been used for centuries as an insecticide and insect repellant. They work well at every stage of the insect's growth, blocking the insect's sodium channels and making their nervous system go haywire! Be warned: pyrethrin works equally on pests and beneficials. Apply with targeted care on your rooftop garden.

Neem. Neem oil, derived from the neem tree (*Azadirachta indica*), is applied in dilution as a foliar spray. It is not instantly fatal, but a hormone disruptor: in any sucking or chewing insects that ingests it, it breaks the cycle of eating, breeding, and, sometimes, flying.

Bacillus thuringiensis (*BT*). This naturally occurring bacteria disrupts the cell walls of insects. Applied as a spray, once ingested it causes the insect's stomach to explode.

Copper. One of the very first fungicides, copper is typically applied as a defense to the leaves of plants affected by fungal pathogens. Copper ions denature proteins, effectively destroying the enzymes that make cells capable of functioning. The spray persists on plant leaves and releases more copper deposits each time the plant gets wet.

Diatomaceous earth (**DE**). Made from the fossilized remains of diatoms (an algae). Works best when dry. Be sure to buy food-grade DE specific to gardening (not the kind you find at a pool supply store).

Homebrewed Pest Controls

Household staples like baking powder, garlic, soap, onions, peppers, oil, and chili pepper flakes are among the many homebrew disease and pest spray ingredients available to rooftop gardeners with a do-it-yourself sensibility. Some of these remedies stand on strong science; others are more the stuff of myth and folklore.

Soaps are a common ingredient in homebrewed pest management blends. If making your own spray, avoid soaps with hand-softening lotions, as well as antibacterial properties. It makes absolutely no sense to apply an antibacterial soap near living soil. Instead, use a milder product like Dr. Bronner's castile soap. I'm fond of the peppermint soap, which has the added benefit of including the powerful pest-repelling volatile oils of mint (while smelling absolutely delicious to me!). Dilute at a ratio of three to six tablespoons to a gallon of water. Soapy water can refract light and burn the leaves of plants; apply a small amount and keep an eye on the plant's reaction for twenty-four hours before applying across the board. A typical negative reaction would be a bleached or burned appearance on the leaves or stem. The plant will usually grow out of the damage. Soaps need to be a reapplied as the pests reappear or after it rains.

As with any other cure, timing and target specificity matters. Be aware that many of these treatments affect beneficials and pests alike. Take care: large doses of chile garlic spray can hurt the gardener as easily as the pest! If I'm spraying a garlic-pepper liquid on my radishes to keep squirrels away, I'm wearing gloves and swim goggles to avoid macing my own eyes. On the rooftop, avoid applying treatments when it's windy.

Record the date, amount, and plants targeted each time you treat them, as you'll likely have to return in a week or two to repeat the process. Finally, don't forget to tell anyone else snacking on, smelling, or gardening the plants what you've been up to!

Recipes for Homebrewed Organic Pest Controls

INSECTICIDAL SOAP

Soaps work against soft-bodied insects such as aphids, chiggers, earwigs, mealybugs, mites, thrips, and whiteflies. Soap works only when sprayed directly on the insects, not once it's dried, so applications must be regular and intentional. To avoid burning the plant leaves, try to apply on overcast days or early in the day, and wash off the plants once the sun rises or emerges from the clouds.

2 tablespoons soap

1 gallon water

Mix gently without making suds. Apply as a spray.

NIGHTSHADE SPRAY

The toxic alkaloids in the leaves of tomatoes, potatoes, eggplants, peppers, and tobacco are naturally occurring pest-repellants that work for these plants while alive, and for you as a pest-management spray! Not only will the spray deter pests, it also attracts some beneficial insects as well. Do not use leaves of diseased plants.

2 to 4 cups nightshade leaves (tomatoes, potatoes, eggplants, peppers, tobacco), roughly chopped

8 cups water, divided

In a bucket with half the water, soak the chopped leaves for 12 to 24 hours. Strain (compost the spent leaves). To the liquid, add the remaining water. Apply as a spray.

GARLIC OIL

The antibacterial properties of garlic protect the clove underground as it grows. Used as a spray, garlic deters all insects indiscriminately, in particular whiteflies, aphids, and many beetles.

4 garlic cloves

2 teaspoons mineral oil

Citrus peel (orange, lemon, lime) to amend the smell (optional)

2 cups water

1 teaspoon dishwashing liquid

Mince the garlic. In a small bowl, mix the garlic and mineral oil. If desired, add citrus peel. Let steep for 24 hours. Strain out the garlic and citrus, and combine the oil, water, and dishwashing liquid. Apply as a spray.

EAGLE STREET ROOFTOP FARM MARKET
TODAY WE ARE SELLI G
GREENS
HONEY
PICKLES
T-SHIRTS

LOOK OUT THIS SEASON FOR
HERBS
SALAD GREEN
UEGGIE

*The making of gardens
and parks goes on with
civilization all over the
world, and they increase
both in size and number as
their value is recognized.
Everybody needs beauty
as well as bread, places
to play in . . . where
Nature may heal and
cheer and give strength to
mind and body alike.*

JOHN MUIR

9

Taking Care of Business

Many of the rooftop farms and gardens featured
in this book follow one of three models: private sites,
onsite above restaurants, and not-for-profit and
school-based production and education spaces.
These are some of the fastest-growing types of
rooftop farms and gardens of the last decade, and
the trend shows no sign of slowing down.

Additionally, there are commercial rooftop farms growing on rooftops across the world. Hydroponic rooftop greenhouses, green roof row farming, and large-scale container systems are all contemporary examples, each with their own crop list and business strategy. In general, high-cost, high-tech strategies have a higher up-front cost but faster payback. For example, Lufa Farms, a rooftop hydroponics greenhouse operation in Canada, spent $71 per square foot to install the garden and projected the run rate revenue as $1.3 million annually, and payback within three years. The Brooklyn Grange Farm, a green roof row farm, cites their first location in Queens at a cost of $5 per square foot to install with a payback period of ten years.

Because of the unique position rooftop farms have in the urban landscape, many who operate them benefit from wearing multiple hats. Produce sales are one element of operations, but many—Eagle Street Rooftop Farm included—have relationships with university and research institutions for the purpose of data collection. Others focus on food aid over profits. I advocate heavily for community education and outreach. Classes, volunteer opportunities, and public engagement are a tremendous benefit of urban farming. Our modern "out of sight, out of mind" attitude about food and farming is likely at the crux of how the food system came to be so broken. By using urban farming as a source of fresh food but also a source of information, it makes more sense at the farmers' market and in the grocery store to support food values that no longer seem abstract from our daily lives. When asked "Can the city feed itself?" I often wonder whether that's the truly important question. Responsible, healthy stewardship of land can happen inside and outside of city landscapes. When we are making our daily food choices, it's far easier to support good food and farming if we participate in the food system as educated consumers—that is to say, rather than focusing on whether the city can feed itself, instead considering whether the city's citizens know *how* to feed themselves.

Using Someone Else's Rooftop

While several of the rooftops featured in this book are private property, many are used with the permission of the building owner. If you're in this position, you should balance your enthusiasm for starting a rooftop garden with a number of desirable characteristics. The most basic walk-through should include an assessment of these elements:

The Rooftop as a Growing Space

Access. Ideally, for ease of installation and use, the rooftop is directly accessible by stairs or an elevator. Find out if these points of egress are up to code. Determine if you will be able to check in on the roof freely throughout the day (or in the middle of the night when a storm is beating up on your chicken coop!).

Preexisting damage. Document and speak to the landlord about any problems with the roof membrane, parapet, and mechanicals. Ask to see the room or rooms below the rooftop, and take a look at the condition of the ceiling and walls.

Irrigation. Check for irrigation points, or where one or several could be run up to the rooftop.

Microclimate. Assess the rooftop's sun exposure, wind, and the effect of shade and glare from nearby buildings.

The Right Relationship with the Building Owner

If you are the non-owner tenant or a rooftop space-seeker, you need the building owner's permission to use the roof. Be prepared to address *their* likely concerns: Will the rooftop garden raise or lower property value? Will it damage the roof? Will it raise the water bill, or help lower energy costs—or both? Will the neighbors complain? What is the increased liability? Aim to enter the conversation prepared with the following items.

A map. A map can be a visual or written document, but it should clearly outline your intentions for the rooftop space. Building code will dictate the legal requirements for points of egress and the height of the parapet wall. Include the access points and parapet height in your design, as well as any pre-existing hardscaping.

A plan for care. If you need to contract a structural engineer, roofers, or other professionals who can ensure proper care for the rooftop, or if you would like the building owner's participation in that process, set that in motion before putting out your plants! You or the building owner should also assess the current condition and needed upgrades to the rooftop's membrane, flashing, parapet walls, and drainage points.

A plan for care extends to your plans and plants. The owner might be concerned about lightweight pots flying around, or weeds, leaves, and rotten tomatoes getting stuck in the drains. Your task is to assure the owner that none of this will happen in your well-cared-for garden.

Your water use. Plant material (even drought-tolerant plants) will need irrigation. Determine if you have rooftop access to water. You can propose to either separate out the water bill or include payment as part of your potential rent for the space. Be prepared to explain your irrigation system and outline how you have planned around weight load issues and prevention of roof membrane damage.

A transition plan. If you don't own the building, eventually you may leave the project. While pitching your concept, outline how you'll pass on the stewardship of the garden or return the rooftop to its original state.

For-Profit Farming

If you are interested in starting a commercial rooftop farm (or a nonprofit with a sales arm, as many of the examples in this book model), here are a few aspects to consider before getting started:

City Code

If you are also interested in selling produce, there are a few items to look into. One is city code, which will determine whether you can legally sell produce and agricultural products like eggs and honey from your rooftop site. If you can, there are likely strict codes about what facilities you must have in place to do so, such as a produce washing station and market-standard scales to weigh the produce.

Funding

Funding sources for starting your rooftop farm can include investors, self-financing, business or personal loans, and equity investments. Many of the models featured in this book used parent companies (such as a restaurant), crowdfunding, and grants by city, state, and federal agencies. The Community Supported Agriculture (CSA) model is an excellent way to prefund your season, once you're up and growing.

Drafting a Business Plan

You should also—if you haven't already—put together a business plan. Begin with the mission and goals of your project. As you describe the dynamics of the business, reassert how it meets personal or organizational and monetary goals, point by point. Address parameters like these:

- Available start-up capital
- Time commitment of the parties involved
- Available space for growing
- Resources needed for growing (for example, water access, growing medium used)
- Market potential

You can also include how your endeavor will impact quality of life, including job creation, environmental impact, community presence, and health and nutrition benefits.

Understanding Your Market

At the Eagle Street Rooftop Farm, we use a handful of traditional farm sales methods to sell our crops. We have an onsite market where visitors can buy directly from us when visiting the rooftop farm. This weekend market allows our customers to connect directly with our produce, right on site. Additionally, throughout the week, we sell off site to chefs at a wholesale price, delivering the produce on foot or by bicycle. As a third point of sale, for a few years we ran a Community Supported Agriculture program. Our CSA model used our rooftop grown produce as well as produce grown by an upstate farmer who previously had no market outlet in New York City. The upstate farm had the capacity to grow a far wider range of produce than our green roof did, and we had the brand name and ready market to get him off and running. I believe that this urban-rural partnership is vital to the success of urban farming. It supplements the gaps on crops that make no financial or horticultural sense to grow in an urban context, and, when a farm partner is chosen well, supports the good land stewardship of small-scale organic farms.

An additional benefit of the CSA model is the ability to accurately track not only produce sales (which we can do with our markets and chef partners) but also household use. Here's what I mean. For grants, publications, and bragging rights, we are often asked how many pounds of produce we grow. It's a difficult question to answer in a way that reflects our real productivity. For example, in the springtime we might grow several hundred pounds of salad greens, whereas in August, when it's too hot to grow lettuces, we might grow twice that poundage in tomatoes. But it's apples and oranges, so to speak: a quarter pound of salad can make enough for two people, while one person could happily scarf down a pound-heavy tomato in a single sitting, or slice up a tomato and have an eighth of a pound as a slice in their sandwich. We found that our Community Supported Agriculture program helped us report how many people we supplied with food and exactly what we supplied them with. The CSA data answered the question of how many pounds of crops we produced annually both as a *quantity* (how many pounds of produce left the rooftop) and for its *quality* (how many households were fed, and what they did with the produce—because we asked!).

UP ON THE ROOF

Higher Ground Farm

BOSTON, MASSACHUSETTS

Founded in 2012

Ninth-story rooftop container garden

Total rooftop space: 10,000 square feet

Total planted space: 2,000 square feet

HigherGroundRooftop Farm.com

In researching, permitting, and fundraising for Higher Ground Farm, a for-profit container-based rooftop farm, experienced ground-level green thumbs John Stoddard and Courtney Hennessey were method-ical and organized in taking their skills to the roof. They knew what they wanted: a minimum of twenty-five thousand square feet, access to water, a good roof membrane, and legal parapet height. An agreeable landlord and a ten-year lease sealed the deal.

Looking for a model with minimal up-front costs and input, they based their container-based farming design on ground-level River Park Farm in New York City. After applying for a short-form permit for temporary and removable use of the rooftop, Stoddard and Hennessey purchased plastic milk crates at $3.50 each, lined the crates with geotextile fabric, and filled them with a bespoke organic growing medium mix.

Within a month, they had financed, purchased, installed, and planted 1,400 containers and started a rooftop farm.

Stoddard and Hennessey used geotextile–fabric lined milk crates to pilot their rooftop farm concept, with the notion—and plenty of remaining available rooftop space—to expand the highly replicable system if their project took off. Some of their best crops so far include microgreens, heirloom tomatoes, and specialized crops such as green coriander seed.

AFTERWORD

At the age of twenty, when I was a very susceptible young thinker, I read Wendell Berry's "The Pleasures of Eating." To this day, it remains the most powerful essay I've ever read about food.

Beginning with the simple assertion that "Eating is an agricultural act," Berry deftly unfolds the tragedy of the modern American food system, then lays out a short charter of actions for the ecological eater. He ties our good health to food sovereignty: the ability to grow our own food, or at least understand where it comes from. He links high quality food to healthy soil, healthy soil to good farming, and better farming stewardship to the sustainability of our watersheds, our country, and our planet. To eat well, he says, is as simple as maintaining a healthy curiosity about the connection between dirt and dinner. The essay concludes with a list of common sense ways an eater can do this. He asks that we cook for ourselves, try to grow our own food, make friends with farmers, and investigate the stories of our favorite plants. I can remember exactly what I did when I finished the article: everything, precisely as he suggested.

Now it is your turn. You'll find that rooftop gardening, urban farming, and farming and gardening in general are challenging tasks. But the word Berry uses—"pleasure"—is an apt counterbalance to this effort. Farming and gardening present opportunities to reengage with a deeply entrenched part of our humanity that goes beyond simply eating well or getting outside. People need plants. In 2005, in the same spring season I started my career at the New York Botanical Garden at its beautiful two-acre family-friendly vegetable gardening site, The Edible Academy, Richard Louv published *Last Child in the Woods*, a call to arms in the face of the rise in obesity, attention deficit disorder, and depression. Regular exposure to nature, Louv suggests, is essential to the health and cognitive development of children and adults alike.

Our personal health and the ecological health of our chosen living environment depends on maintaining and creating new green spaces. This is particularly true as internationally we become a more urban people. All rooftops—in and outside of cities—could be greener, but markedly in the density of an urban landscape, rooftop gardens and green roofs have transformative power. In 2009, the year we founded the Eagle Street Rooftop Farm, an abandoned elevated train track in Manhattan's Chelsea neighborhood opened in renewed use as the High Line. It quickly became one of the most popular public parks of the last century, welcoming five million visitors a year.

Rooftop farming is a thread in a larger woven landscape we've spent a long time unraveling but can yet stitch back together. Whether it's food, pleasure, entrepreneurship, health, community, or necessity that brings you up to the roof, your efforts are a note in a long-sung song. Indeed, when looking at the landscape of empty rooftops around you and wondering where to begin, it's important to remember the stubbornness of nature below and above our architecture. In New York City, I see it in the weeds prying up through sidewalk cracks, or in the red-tailed hawks circling their way back into an ecosystem by nesting in the stone facades of turn-of-the-century buildings. In the years the High Line sat fallow, wildflowers grew up through the train trusses. There's a necessity to green spaces, which in his poem *In a Country Once Forested* Berry gently reminds us is as inevitable as we allow it to be:

> . . . *the soil under the grass*
> *is dreaming of a young forest,*
>
> *and under the pavement the soil*
> *is dreaming of grass.*

Say yes to the hearty adventure!
JOSEPH CAMPBELL

APPENDIX

Before you climb up the stairs and get growing, it's useful to research a quick sketch of preliminary parameters of what's permissible for your rooftop site. The questions below also address resources (like soil testing and water quality) and regulations around sales and animals (if either venture is of interest!).

Rooftop Regulations

- What permits are needed to do a green roof, greenhouse, or container garden on a rooftop?

- Are there any existing available tax abatements/credits? (If of interest, are there any additional green infrastructure—solar panels, white roofing, etc.— tax abatements/credits?)

- What is the required legal parapet height for a rooftop garden, green roof, or greenhouse installation?

- What is the requirement for egress?

- What are the fire code requirements around rooftop gardening (including setback, egress, materials used)?

Irrigation

- Is greywater use legal?

- Is storm water collection (rain barrel use) legal?

- What type of water does the city have (hard/soft) and what is its source? Is the pH identified?

Soil

- What is the best local resource for soil testing (including local cooperative extensions/universities)? Do they offer plant tissue testing, to identify buildup of pollutants in the plants themselves?

Food sales/packaging

- What are the regulations for sale of fresh produce?

- What are the regulations for sale of packaged products?

- Does this vary between land zoning (private, public, agricultural etc.)?

Animals

- Is beekeeping legal?

- Is raising laying hens legal? What does local code specify about the number of hens and habitat structure?

RESOURCES

This book has a helpful companion site, rooftopgrowingguide.com. Below are other sources I have found helpful.

Books

BIRDS AND BEES

Berenbaum, May R. *The Earwig's Tail: A Modern Bestiary of Multi-Legged Legends.* Cambridge, MA: Harvard University Press, 2009.

Bradley, Fern M., Barbara W. Ellis, and Deborah L. Martin. *The Organic Gardener's Handbook of Natural Pest and Disease Control.* New York: Rodale, 2009.

Gillman, Jeff. *The Truth about Garden Remedies: What Works, What Doesn't, & Why.* Portland, OR: Timber Press, 2006.

Hoyt, Murray. *The World of Bees.* New York: Bonanza Books, 1965.

Lee-Mader, Eric, Jennifer Hopwood, Lora Morandin, Mace Vaughan, and Scott Hoffman Black. *Farming with Native Beneficial Insects.* North Adams, MA: Storey Publishing, 2014.

Mader, Eric, Matthew Shepherd, Mace Vaughan, Scott H. Black, and Gretchen LeBuhn. *Attracting Native Pollinators: Protecting North America's Bees and Butterflies.* North Adams, MA: Storey Publishing, 2011.

Martin, Deborah L. *Best-Ever Backyard Birding Tips: Hundreds of Easy Ways to Attract the Birds You Love to Watch.* New York: Rodale Inc., 2008.

Paska, Megan. *The Rooftop Beekeeper: A Scrappy Guide to Keeping Honeybees.* San Francisco, CA: Chronicle Books, 2014.

Sammataro, Diana, and Alphonse Avitabile. *The Bee-keeper's Handbook.* 3rd ed. Ithaca, NY: Comstock Publishing Associates, 1998.

Schultz, Warren, ed. *Natural Insect Control: The Ecological Gardener's Guide to Foiling Pests.* Brooklyn, NY: Brooklyn Botanic Garden, 1999.

FLOWERS AND HERBS

Byczynski, Lynn. *The Flower Farmer: An Organic Grower's Guide to Raising and Selling Cut Flowers.* White River Junction, VT: Chelsea Green Publishing, 2008.

Gilbertie, Sal, and Lauren Jarrett. *Herb Gardening from the Ground Up: Everything You Need to Know About Growing Your Favorite Herbs.* Berkeley, CA: Ten Speed Press, 2012.

Orr, Stephen. *The New American Herbal.* New York: Clarkson Potter Publishers, 2014.

GREENHOUSE GROWING

Beckett, Kenneth A. *Growing Under Glass.* London: Mitchell Beazley, 1999.

Coleman, Eliot. *Four-Season Harvest: Organic Vegetables from Your Home Garden All Year Long.* White River Junction, VT: Chelsea Green Publishing Company, 1999.

Coleman, Eliot. *The Winter Harvest Handbook: Year-Round Vegetable Production Using Deep-Organic Techniques and Unheated Greenhouses.* White River Junction, VT: Chelsea Green Publishing Company, 2009.

Marshall, Roger. *The Greenhouse Gardener's Manual.* Portland, OR: Timber Press, 2014.

Smith, Shane. *Greenhouse Gardener's Companion: Growing Food and Flowers in Your Greenhouse or Sunspace.* Golden, CO: Fulcrum Publishing, 2000.

MARKET GARDENING AND FARMING

Hansen, Ann L. *The Organic Farming Manual: A Comprehensive Guide to Starting and Running a Certified Organic Farm.* North Adams, MA: Storey Publishing, 2010.

Lee, Andrew W. *Backyard Market Gardening: The Entrepreneur's Guide to Selling What You Grow.* Columbus, NC: Good Earth Publications, 1996.

Plakias, Anastasia Cole. *The Farm on the Roof: What Brooklyn Grange Taught Us About Entrepreneurship Community, and Growing a Sustainable Business.* New York: Avery, 2016.

Stewart, Keith. *Storey's Guide to Growing Organic Vegetables & Herbs for Market.* North Adams, MA: Storey Publishing, 2013.

ROOFTOPS, BALCONIES, GREEN ROOFS, URBAN LANDSCAPES, AND HYDROPONICS

Carpenter, Novella, and Willow Rosenthal. *The Essential Urban Farmer.* New York: Penguin Books, 2011.

Dakin, Karla, Lisa L. Benjamin, and Mindy Pantiel. *The Professional Design Guide to Green Roofs.* Portland, OR: Timber Press, 2013.

Dunnett, Nigel, Dusty Gedge, John Little, and Edmund C. Snodgrass. *Small Green Roofs: Low-Tech Options for Greener Living.* Portland, OR: Timber Press, 2011.

Hanson, Beth, and Sarah Schmidt, eds. *Green Roofs and Rooftop Gardens.* Brooklyn, NY: Brooklyn Botanic Garden, 2012.

Luckett, Kelly. *Green Roof Construction and Maintenance.* New York: McGraw-Hill, 2009.

Mandel, Lauren. *Eat Up: The Inside Scoop on Rooftop Agriculture.* Gabriola Island, BC: New Society Publishers, 2013.

Mitchell, Alex. *The Edible Balcony: Growing Fresh Produce in the Heart of the City.* London: Kyle Cathie Limited, 2010.

Roberto, Keith. *How-To Hydroponics.* Farmingdale, NY: Futuregarden Press, 2005.

Snodgrass, Edmund C., and Linda McIntyre. *The Green Roof Manual: A Professional Guide to Design, Installation, and Maintenance.* Portland, OR: Timber Press, 2010.

Weiler, Susan K., and Katrin Scholz-Barth. *Green Roof Systems: A Guide to Planning, Design, and Construction of Landscapes over Structure.* Hoboken, NJ: Wiley, 2009.

SOIL, NUTRIENTS, ECOSYSTEMS, AND COMPOSTING

Bodanis, David. *The Secret Garden: Dawn to Dusk in the Astonishing Hidden World of the Garden.* New York: Simon & Schuster, 1992.

Dunne, Nial, ed. *Healthy Soils for Sustainable Gardens.* Brooklyn, NY: Brooklyn Botanic Garden, 2009.

Hanson, Beth, ed. *Easy Compost: The Secret to Great Soil and Spectacular Plants.* Brooklyn, NY: Brooklyn Botanic Garden, 1997.

Lowenfels, Jeff. *Teaming with Nutrients: The Organic Gardener's Guide to Optimizing Plant Nutrition.* Portland, OR: Timber Press, 2013.

Lowenfels, Jeff, and Wayne Lewis. *Teaming with Microbes: The Organic Gardener's Guide to the Soil Food Web.* Portland, OR: Timber Press, 2010.

Nardi, James B. *Life in the Soil: A Guide for Naturalists and Gardeners.* Chicago: The University of Chicago Press, 2007.

Pleasant, Barbara, and Deborah L. Martin. *The Complete Compost Gardening Guide.* North Adams, MA: Storey Publishing, 2008.

Stamets, Paul. *Mycelium Running: How Mushrooms Can Help Save the World.* Berkeley, CA: Ten Speed Press, 2005.

Stell, Elizabeth P. *Secrets to Great Soil.* Pownal, VT: Storey Communications, 1998.

STYLES AND SYSTEMS OF VEGETABLE GROWING

Akeroyd, Simon. *Kitchen Gardening for Beginners: A Simple Guide to Growing Fruits and Vegetables.* New York: DK Publishing, 2013.

Bartholomew, Mel. *All New Square Foot Gardening: The Revolutionary Way to Grow More in Less Space.* Minneapolis, MN: Cool Springs Press, 2013.

Coleman, Eliot. *The New Organic Grower: A Master's Manual of Tools and Techniques for the Home and Market Gardener.* White River Junction, VT: Chelsea Green Publishing, 1995.

Flowerdew, Bob. *The No-Work Garden: Getting the Most Out of Your Garden for the Least Amount of Work.* London: Kyle Cathie Limited, 2002.

Jabbour, Niki. *Groundbreaking Food Gardens: 73 Plans That Will Change the Way You Grow Your Garden.* North Adams, MA: Storey Publishing, 2014.

Jeavons, John. *How to Grow More Vegetables: And Fruits, Nuts, Berries, Grains, and Other Crops Than You Ever Thought Possible on Less Land Than You Can Imagine.* Berkeley, CA: Ten Speed Press, 2006.

Martin, Deborah L. *Rodale's Basic Organic Gardening: A Beginner's Guide to Starting a Healthy Garden.* New York: Rodale Press, 2014.

Newcomb, Karen. *The Postage Stamp Vegetable Garden: Grow Tons of Organic Vegetables in Tiny Spaces and Containers.* Berkeley, CA: Ten Speed Press, 2015.

Peavy, Dr. William S., and Warren Peary. *Super Nutrition Gardening: How to Grow Your Own Powercharged Foods.* Garden City Park, NY: Avery Publishing Group, 1993.

Pleasant, Barbara. *Starter Vegetable Gardens: 24 No-Fail Plans for Small Organic Gardens.* North Adams, MA: Storey Publishing, 2010.

THE BASICS: BOTANY AND SEEDS

Bubel, Nancy. *The New Seed-Starters Handbook.* Emmaus, PA: Rodale Press, 1988.

Capon, Brian. *Botany for Gardeners: An Introduction and Guide.* Portland, OR; Timber Press, 1990.

Elpel, Thomas J. *Botany in a Day: Herbal Field Guide to Plant Families.* Pony, MT: HOPS Press, 2001.

Essential Atlas of Botany. Hauppauge, NY: Barron's Educational Series, 2004.

Greenwood, Pippa. *Basic Gardening.* New York: DK Publishing, 1998.

Rothman, Julia. *Farm Anatomy: The Curious Parts & Pieces of Country Life.* North Adams, MA: Storey Publishing, 2011.

Taylor, Barbara. *Incredible Plants.* New York: DK Publishing, 1997.

Young, Paul. *The Botany Coloring Book.* New York: HarperCollins, 1982.

THE STORIES THAT SHAPE US

Berry, Wendell. *The Unsettling of America: Culture & Agriculture.* San Francisco, CA: Sierra Club Books, 1996.

Dillard, Annie. *Pilgrim at Tinker Creek.* New York: Harper's Magazine Press, 1974.

Gorgolewski, Mark, June Komisar, and Joe Nasr. *Carrot City: Creating Places for Urban Agriculture.* New York: Monacelli Press, 2011.

Gussow, Joan. *Growing, Older: A Chronicle of Death, Life, and Vegetables.* Burlington, VT: Chelsea Green, 2010.

Jackson, Wes. *Consulting the Genius of the Place: An Ecological Approach to New Agriculture.* Berkeley, CA: Counterpoint, 2010.

Kirschenmann, Frederick L. *Cultivating an Ecological Conscience: Essays from a Farmer Philosopher.* Berkeley, CA: Counterpoint, 2010.

Orr, Stephen. *Tomorrow's Garden: Design and Inspiration for a New Age of Sustainable Gardening.* New York: Rodale Press, 2011.

Pollan, Michael. *Second Nature: A Gardener's Education.* New York: Grove Press, 1991.

Pretor-Pinney, Gavin. *The Cloudspotter's Guide: The Science, History, and Culture of Clouds.* New York: Perigee, 2006.

Sanderson, Eric W. *Terra Nova: The New World After Oil, Cars, and Suburbs.* New York: Abrams, 2013.

Stewart, Keith. *It's a Long Road to a Tomato: Tales of an Organic Farmer Who Quit the Big City for the (Not So) Simple Life.* New York: Marlowe & Company, 2006.

TREES

Crosbie, Colin. *Easy Pruning.* New York: DK Publishing, 2007.

Heriteau, Jacqueline. *Complete Trees, Shrubs, & Hedges.* Upper Saddle River, NJ: Creative Homeowner, 2006.

Peattie, Donald C. *A Natural History of North American Trees.* San Antonio, TX: Trinity University Press, 2013.

Roddick, Christopher, and Beth Hanson. *The Tree Care Primer.* Brooklyn, NY: Brooklyn Botanic Garden, 2007.

WEEDS

Martin, Alexander C. *Weeds.* New York: St. Martin's Press, 1987.

Pfeiffer, Ehrenfried E. *Weeds and What They Tell Us.* Edinburgh: Floris Books, 2012.

Websites

Online resources are constantly changing, but here are a few that can help you get growing:

Eatupag.com
   Eat Up: a blog dedicated to rooftop agriculture

Greenroofs.com
   Green Roofs and Green Wall Database

Greenroofs.org
   Green Roofs for Healthy Cities

NYFEA.org
   National Young Farmers Association

NOAA.gov
   National Oceanic and Atmospheric Association

Rooftopfarms.org
   The Eagle Street Rooftop Farm

USDA.gov
   The United States Department of Agriculture

Xerces.org
   The Xerces Society for Invertibrate Conservation

Seed Companies

harrisseeds.com
   Harris Seeds

highmowingseeds.com
   High Mowing Seeds

johnnyseeds.com
   Johnny's Selected Seeds

plantsofthesouthwest.com
   Plants of the Southwest

rareseeds.com
   Baker's Creek Heirloom Seeds

seedlibrary.org
   Hudson Valley Seed Library

seedsavers.org
   Seed Savers Exchange

turtletreeseed.org
   Turtle Tree Seed

INDEX

Copyright © 2016 by Annie Novak
Illustrations copyright © 2016 Annie Novak and Lauren Heanes

All rights reserved.
Published in the United States by Ten Speed Press, an imprint of the
Crown Publishing Group, a division of Penguin Random House LLC, New York.
www.crownpublishing.com
www.tenspeed.com

Ten Speed Press and the Ten Speed Press colophon are registered trademarks
of Penguin Random House LLC.

Photographs on pages ii, vi, x, 14, 19, 23, 24, 31, 33, 42, 43, 45, 47, 49, 60, 93,
97, 129, 133, 145, 151, 156, 160, 163, 172, 180, 181, 184, 188, 196, 205, 210, 211,
212, 213, 215, 218, 219, 220, 221, 224, and 239 © 2016 by Annie Novak.

Photographs on pages iv, vi, vii, x, 1, 6, 8, 17, 21, 23, 24, 31, 33, 39, 40, 43, 47,
48, 49, 53, 55, 59, 60, 62, 63, 64, 67, 72, 73, 75, 76, 77, 79, 80, 81, 82, 83, 84,
85, 88, 96, 115, 117, 127, 128, 131, 139, 141, 148, 151, 154, 162, 168, 180, 183,
196, 197, 198, 221, 224, and 236 © 2016 by Naima Green.

Photographs on pages v, 52, 68, 70, 71, 110, 132, 141, 143, 183, 187, and 233
© 2016 by Jackie Snow.

Photographs on pages 39 and 159 © 2016 by Mark K. Morrison.

Photograph on page 46 © 2016 by Fritz Haeg.

Photograph on page 95 © 2016 by David Haddad.

Library of Congress Cataloging–in–Publication Data
Novak, Annie, 1983– author.
 The rooftop growing guide : how to transform your roof into a vegetable
garden or farm / Annie Novak ; photography by Naima Green and Jackie Snow ;
illustration by Annie Novak and Lauren Heanes. — First edition.
    pages cm
Includes bibliographical references and index.
 1. Roof gardening. 2. Urban gardening. I. Title.
SB419.5.N68 2016
635.9'671—dc23
                          2015025842

Trade Paperback ISBN: 978–1–60774–708–6
eBook ISBN: 978–1–60774–709–3

Printed in China

Design by Betsy Stromberg

10 9 8 7 6 5 4 3 2 1

First Edition